The Football Grounds of
Essex Metropolitan

b̥

LEYTON FOOTBALL CLUB. OPENING MATCH SEPT 1st 1905.

Photography by Jon Weaver, except where indicated

Series Editor: Mike Floate   Designed by Colin Peel & Mike Floate   Series Consultant: Colin Peel

Published by Newlands Printing Services, Newlands Cottages, Stones Cross Road,
Crockenhill, Swanley, Kent BR8 8LX

© Jon Weaver & Mike Floate2006

British Library Cataloguing in Publication Data.
A catalogue record for this volume is available from the British Library.

Photo above: A Postcard showing Leyton FC's first game at Osbourne Road in September 1905.
Note the box camera on a tripod to the right of the near corner flag.
Front Cover: from top left... AFC Hornchurch, Leyton Orient, Clapton, Purfleet, Leyton, West Ham United.
Back cover: from top... Romford, Dagenham & Redbridge, Manford Way FC, Sterling Athletic.

ISBN 978-1-900257-16-9

Printed and bound by Catford Print Centre (020 8695 0101)

Introduction

This book is the companion to 'The Football Grounds of Rural Essex', published in October 2005. My intention with these two books has been to alert the reader to a number of smaller football grounds throughout the county of Essex and into East London. There is a great deal of hidden history to unearth, and I hope that I have been successful in doing so.... not least the school field in Snaresbrook which has hosted an F.A. Cup Quarter Final!

The dividing line used to separate the two volumes has been the M25 - those inside being Metropolitan. This book has a different feel to its predecessor as villages become few and far between and more and more teams utilise larger sports centres and playing fields. Many of the teams featured here can be found along Forest Road which stretches from Barkingside, through Fairlop to Hainault. Leyton weighs in with five entries and Romford, Dagenham, Barking and East Ham each have their quota of clubs.

The East End of London is of course home to the world famous Hackney Marshes and there is enough secret history there to justify inclusion. That whole area around Hackney, Leyton and Stratford is soon to be regenerated as development of the 2012 Olympic Stadium gets underway. Work now turns to the final book in the trilogy – one which undertakes to cover all of the former football grounds covering the whole Essex & East London region. There are a lot of them, so expect plenty of gems to be unearthed, going back over a hundred years in some cases.

Some of the grounds intended for that book have been moved forward to this one to keep the size manageable, and in doing so I have had to move the goalposts slightly. This book therefore includes what could have been classed as 'lost' Metropolitan grounds which actually still exist *and* have football being played on them at some rudimentary level. Hence, Barkingside's former Recreation Ground home is here but listed under the current incumbents, Crowmill F.C. Also here are all the old London Spartan League grounds still in use by park teams, a former Essex Senior League venue for East Thurrock United, a former ground for Millwall when they played north of the river in the Southern League (as Millwall Athletic).

The regularity with which clubs in the vicinity change ground or name can be very confusing and I have therefore added two glossaries to the back of the book so that the reader can maintain their bearings.

My grateful thanks are extended once again to everyone that has helped me with my cries for help, they are all acknowledged opposite and my sincere apologies to anyone who has inadvertently been omitted. Special thanks to my young son, Scott, who has accompanied me on many of my photographic missions and who has hopefully developed an everlasting bond with Braintree Town F.C. during the 2005/06 season.

Jon Weaver
Braintree, Essex, September 2006

Acknowledgements

The following people have helped with research for this book: Vince Taylor, Paul Claydon, Scott Weaver, Gavin Ellis, Nigel Upson, Richard Brock, Len Llewellyn, Peter Miles, James Wright, Bob Lilliman, Alasdair Ross, Roger Adams, Mike Floate, Colin Peel, Ed West, Arthur Numpton, Billy Bamforth.

Chris Mawson (Simmons Aerofilms), Robert Errington, (Esex Senior League), Peter Godfrey (Essex Olympian League), Simon Inglis & Alastair Gaff (Malavan Models), Ray Harrison (Eastern Junior Alliance) Tom Miller (National UK 5-A-Side Championships).

Keith Campen (Loughton F.C.), Peter Butcher (Romford Recorder), John Zeraschi (Hackney Marshes), Tony Incenzo (Talk Sport Radio), Gary Pettit (Faces F.C.), Rob Craven, Chris Evans and Phil Sammons (Essex F.A.), Matt Porter (Leyton Orient), Dr. Tim Grose (UK Running Track Directory), Simon O'Connor, Nick Hayes, Waltham Forest Oral History Workshop, David Pracy, Terry Hurley, Alan Chandler, Steve Lawson (Aveley F.C.), Val Bryant (Redbridge Libraries), Ilford Times, Romford Times, Leyton Gazette & Guardian, Vestry House Museum.

Abbreviations used throughout this book:

Leagues referred to by unsponsored names

EBHL	Essex Business Houses League
EJA	Eastern Junior Alliance
EOL	Essex Olympian League
ESL	Essex Senior League
IDL	Ilford & District League
LSL	London Spartan League
MCL	Middlesex County League

I have tried wherever possible to list a ground under the most senior club currently playing there. On a number of occasions the clubs listed in the second half of the book may be unfamiliar to the reader e.g. St. Vincents of the Ilford & District League are now the highest placed club playing at the Leyton County Ground.

Dedicated to Scott Weaver

Feedback, comments and queries welcome to: jon.weaver1@btinternet.com

Scott Weaver and the upturned dugouts on the second pitch at M&B Club, in Dagenham.

Aveley F.C.

Millfield, Mill Road,
Aveley,
RM15 4TR

The club moved to Mill Field in 1952 and supporters set about lovingly building the ground up, with a large bank of terracing along one side that has survived to this day in remarkably good condition.

The original changing rooms were on this side. A small stand was obtained for £100 from Grays Athletic and still stands opposite the terracing, being known as the Pepper Stand. Over the years the roof and back wall have both been replaced, so essentially it is just the wooden supports and the four concrete steps within that have stood the test of time.

When the Foster family invested £19,000 in the club, radical ground improvements were forthcoming. A new 100ft long grandstand, costing £2600, rose up on the top of the terracing in 1958, with allowance made for the possibility of future extensions. Floodlights were installed on the training pitch behind the Pepper Stand, and extra terracing was laid. In 1959 supporters set about raising funds for a large clubhouse behind the south goal, with a lounge bar, offices and a committee room.

Aveley F.C.

Floodlights were first used on the main pitch for the local derby with Grays in 1967. The record attendance of 2,623 was posted in 1978 for an F.A. Cup tie with Wycombe Wanderers.

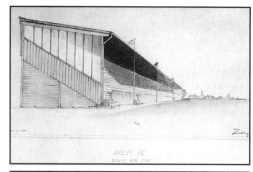

Today the ground is little changed although Isthmian ground grading requirements were responsible for seeing each end truncated to a narrow pathway, with very limited terracing. The grandstand still dominates the ground and offers fine views over the industrious Thames Estuary, particularly at night. The clubs name was brightly painted in four foot high letters on the back wall, although these days they are in need of another coat.

The stand still has a grass paddock, fronted by a white wicker fence, a wonderful survivor from the glory days. There are 340 tip-up seats for spectators, and they all have a good view of the pitch with minimal disruption from the four narrow roof supports.

Top: An artist's impression of the new stand before construction in 1958.
Photo: Steve Lawson Collection
Above: The finished stand in 1958.
Photo: Steve Lawson Collection.
Below: The stand in 2004. So little has changed at Aveley over the years!

The large press box has two steep rows of padded seats, and with its glass screen frontage looks very impressive. In front of this is the Directors Box. Originally the whole of this central section comprised tip up seats, with the rest being bench seating.

Aveley F.C.

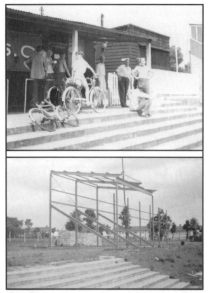

Top: The new supporters club tea bar 1958. Above: The new stand under construction 1958. All Photos: Steve Lawson Collection.

Top: Preparation of the new ground 1952. Above: Volunteers working on the terracing and the site of the stand 1958.

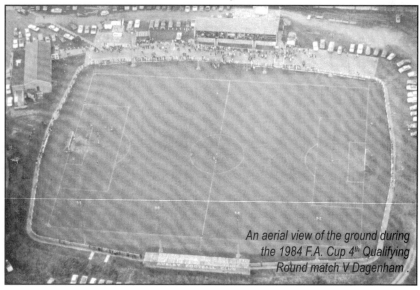

An aerial view of the ground during the 1984 F.A. Cup 4th Qualifying Round match V Dagenham .

Barking F.C.

Mayesbrook Park, Lodge Avenue, Barking, RM8 2JH

The Main Stand in 2004.

The ground had been an open park/ sports field for many years, with various small shelters dotted throughout. One of these used to stand quite near the North West corner of the current ground. On 1st September 1951 the athletics stadium opened, with its classic grandstand (how the football club must wish they could swap it for their own!).

Barking F.C. moved in to the field next door much later, in 1973, bringing their floodlight pylons with them from Vicarage Field. Cover was originally provided on the north side by a temporary trailer stand. This was removed when the current low stand, similar to that at Canvey, was built. At first there was seating provision for 210 and adjacent standing cover for 450. In more recent times the seating has been updated with three rows of red tip-up seats.

Right: Narrow terracing within the main stand in 2004.

Barking F.C.

Above: The clubhouse end terrace in 1988. Photo. Richard Brock
Right: The re-profiled clubhouse end terrace and the 2001 cover.
Right lower: The original, and temporary, trailer stand. Photo: Bob Lilliman

The clubhouse is behind the near goal, with a broad section of uncovered terracing at this end which was upgraded and covered in 2001, when Barking merged with East Ham United. The two other sides of the ground remain flat standing. In April 2004 the club was granted £59,300 to replace fencing and the old floodlights.

The record attendance stands at 1,972 V Aldershot in the 2nd Round of the F.A. Cup in 1978.

Barkingside F.C.

Oakside Stadium,
Station Road,
Barkingside, IG6 1NB

Any lovers of architecture who alight from the Central Line at Barkingside Station en route to Oakside, should pause a while to admire the wondrous old station with its wrought iron castings, dogtooth fascia, and roof-top cupola, for there is precious little of beauty upon arrival at Oakside. That said, the ground is quite fascinating, and is currently on its third makeover with another to follow if a bid for a new grandstand ever succeeds.

The lease of this ground has belonged to groundsharers Redbridge F.C. since 2001, but it will be a long time before the ground is considered as anything other than Barkingside's. Preparation on the ground began in 1956, involving the removal of large concrete tank traps, a legacy from WWII, and also the diversion of a brook around the ground. Some of the traps remained into the 1980s.

The first game took place on Saturday 24th August 1957, a London League fixture with Cray Wanderers. The ground was banked up on three sides, and it was intended that 15 ft terraces would be developed and a large 600 seat grandstand would be built with changing rooms underneath and additional cover opposite. The capacity would have been 10,000, but the plans were never realised. There was a covered lean-to area on top of the bank, catering for 100, which backed onto the tube station.

Left: The early lean-to cover on the bank at the station side January 1978. Photo: Bob Lilliman
Above: The crude breeze block replacement, seen in 1980. Photo: Bob Lilliman

Barkingside F.C.

A fire in the early 1970s forced the club to play at Woodford Avenue (see the forthcoming 'Lost Grounds of Essex & East London') until the present clubhouse was built. In 1976 the Essex Senior League turned aside an application for admission to the league, and then at the end of the 1970s the cover made way for a very small roughly hewn breezeblock shelter. Corner floodlights on poles were erected in the summer of 1989.

There have been a number of short-lived stands at the ground. The current main stand is on the site of the earlier shelters and a temporary structure, and is itself an extension of an earlier format. On the opposite side a small uncovered seated stand was quickly replaced by a much larger version, still uncovered but holding 250. It didn't have planning permission, so was soon removed.

A penalty area-width terraced cover, five steps deep, behind the near goal suffered the same fate in 2002. On 19th November 2003 Redbridge's predecessors Ford United entertained Port Vale in an F.A. Cup 1st Round replay, with a lower than anticipated crowd of 1,374 shoehorned into the tiny ground.

Photos - top right to bottom:
1) The current (fifth) stand on the station side, October 2003.
2) A short lived uncovered stand on the far side, 1998. Photo: Vince Taylor
3) Cover no.4 on the station side, March 1999. Photo: Vince Taylor
4) The third cover on the station side, Sept 1998. Photo: Vince Taylor
5) The car park end terrace, 2003.

Barkingside F.C.

Currently there is a wide raised terrace either side of the seated stand and a pitch-width one behind the near goal. A low pitch-length cover is on the opposite side, with evidence of the old banking now marooned behind it. This had started out as a short shelter, four uprights long, in a central position. There is a simple and narrow standing area at the far end.

This is a ground crying out for a replacement to the scaffold-pole and tin sheeting stand that somehow passed Conference South grading requirements in 2004. That one has not been forthcoming so far speaks volumes for the local authority.

Top: The main stand. *Above*: The side terrace. *Below*: Panoramic view of Oakside, Aug. 2003. Photos: Colin Peel

Clapton F.C.

Old Spotted Dog Ground,
Upton Lane,
Forest Gate, E7 9NP

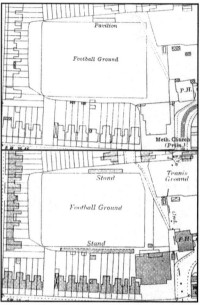

The legend of the Old Spotted Dog ground, home to Clapton since 1888, has always been greater than reality. It had previously been used by St. Bartholomew's Hospital and had a small entrance in Upton Lane. It takes its name from the historic old pub on the main road, which sadly closed in December 2004. It was rumoured to have originally been Henry VIII's hunting dog kennels. Taking up the hospital team's lease, Clapton's first game there was a very creditable 1-0 victory over Old Carthusians. Cricket was played there until WWI, and the space around the ground in those days allowed temporary stands to be built to cater for an astonishing crowd of 12,000 for the visit of Tottenham Hotspur.

Above: Two OS Maps, 1920 (top) and 1939 (above) showing the stand and terrace built between the wars.

Clapton F.C.

As a leading light in the Southern League the club was able to attract gates of up to 4,000 on a regular basis. The club won the F.A. Amateur Cup no less than five times during a glorious period either side of WWI. This was in spite of, rather than because of the ground which was never developed to the extent of a number of other non-League stadiums in the capital. At the outset there was no cover and the large crowds were kept back by a rope. A barn with no running water acted as a changing room. In wet weather, hard standing was provided around the ground by breaking up wooden crates and laying down the sides. A small member's stand was provided which catered for four members of the press.

A separate press box was soon built, and the small stand burnt down in the 1920s to be replaced by a wooden grandstand on one side with a sloping roof and raised seating deck which was reached by some short steps. By this time a pitch-length covered timber terrace stood opposite and each end had a cinder terrace that was open to the elements. The playing surface was surrounded by a traditional white wicker fence and changing facilities were in the corner nearest the pub.

Effectively while other clubs moved on, Clapton became stuck in a time warp and by the early 1990s the old wooden stands were in a perilous state and crowds rarely reached three figures. Half of the grandstand had been demolished and much of the truncated terraced cover had been blown backwards against the fencing and trees of the gardens beyond.

The full length main stand, shortly after it lost its 'WATNEYS ALES' advert from the roof. 1979. Photo: Bob Lilliman

Top: The sorry remains of the old main stand. April 1994.

Clapton F.C.

To survive, the club had to remove the stands and start again. Over the years the club has said many goodbyes to the Old Spotted Dog but like a faithful old friend always comes back for more, surviving many scares. During WWII they gave up the lease and moved to the Port of London Authority ground at Ilford. A spell away in the 1990s is commemorated in the bar with a plaque marking Clapton's return home on 12th November 1994 and then in 2001/02 they did not play a single game there, hiring out grounds at Aveley, Purfleet, Wembley, Hertford and Barking & East Ham.

Above The covered terrace opposite the stand. Photo: Bob Lilliman Below: The partially destroyed timber terrace in April 1994.

The lack of money for this club, in a deprived area of East London, is evident everywhere. Admission money is collected on a table while a pay box a little further on is littered with rubbish and unused. The portakabin behind it has been burned out.

On the left is a modern 100 seat stand with no side panels and therefore very exposed to the elements. Opposite is a delightfully quirky little section of cover. It has a central stairway leading to an elevated platform, and the roof also extends over the front. It has a blank fascia board and looks utterly fascinating. The far end is an overgrown bank, with two terraced steps behind the goal and a pair of crush barriers. At the other end is a smaller overgrown bank.

Above: A small terrace at the far end, to satisfy Isthmian League regulations.
Below: The replacement cover on the site of the old main stand. Sept 1995.
Photo: Richard Brock

Without a benefactor it is difficult to imagine either the club or ground surviving another ten years without having an active set of supporters to mobilise.

Dagenham & Redbridge F.C.

Glyn Hopkin Stadium,
Victoria Road,
Dagenham, RM10 7XL

The land upon which the current stadium stands was originally part of Wantz Farm. In 1910 the Sterling Telephone & Electric Co. Ltd opened their factory next door, and occasional inter-company games were played before the football ground was officially opened in 1920 for use by Sterling Athletic F.C.

As early as February 1921 4,000 watched an Essex Senior Cup tie between Leytonstone and Barking, after Leytonstone's ground was closed because of crowd disturbances. Sterling played in the London League until 1924 and then in local football until the factory closed in 1931. The ground during their tenure was neatly staked off but there had been no covered accommodation.

Briggs Motor Bodies F.C. took over the factory and ground in 1932. They initially moved the pitch 90 degrees but returned it to where it is today after WWII. There was a pavilion with changing rooms at the Victoria Road end of ground and a small scaffold stand on the factory side with grass banking, but little terracing. The south side was open so that cricket, baseball etc. could be played during the summer.

Above: A 1950 sketch of the ground from The Romford Times. *Below*: An aerial view from April 1921, when it was home to Sterling Athletic. Amazingly, a crowd of 4,000 had watched a game here just two months earlier. Photo: Aerofilms Ref. 5611

Dagenham & Redbridge F.C.

In 1949 Briggs transported an old American Army Nissen hut from Devon and erected it as a clubhouse behind the Victoria Road goal. On October 13th 1951 the host club, now known as Briggs Sports, met Romford in the F.A. Cup 2nd Qualifying Round. A crowd exceeding 12,000 was anticipated so on police advice they made the game all ticket and limited the attendance to 5,000. To help accommodate everyone an extra stand was installed, normally used for baseball. This brought the seating up to between 300 and 400 and they also installed wooden terracing which later moved with them to their new ground at Rush Green in 1955.

Above: The former Brigg stand, seen during the first year of Dagenham's occupation in 1955-56. The pitched roof of the factory behind makes the cover look far grander than it was!

Above: The famous Amateur Cup Quarter Final tie in 1954 when Briggs beat the holders Pegasus 3-0 showing part of the small stand.

The council then awarded a 28-year lease at £350 p.a. to Dagenham F.C. and they took over the 5.5 acre ground on 24th May 1955 after rejecting Glebe Road. The club had previously played at Dagenham Arena. There was much work to do and in a short spell they fully enclosed and levelled the pitch, re-seeded and removed stones, extended banking and terracing to accommodate 10,000, built turnstiles, and a new car park prepared partly on the old tennis courts and bowling green. The centrepiece of the ground became a new 660-seat wooden grandstand. It was 60 yards long, and had a paddock area for a further 345 standing spectators. It was opened on 7th January 1956 by Mr. J W Bowers, the Chairman of Essex F.A.

DAGENHAM
FOOTBALL CLUB
Official Programme   35p

Sponsored throughout
the 1985-86 Season by

Kettering Town
GOLA LEAGUE
Saturday 28 September 1985
Kick-off 3 p.m.

Dagenham & Redbridge F.C.

In the summer of 1957 concrete terracing was laid behind the Victoria Road goal, and turnstiles were built at the Pondfield Park end. The first set of floodlights were first used in 1957, and were superseded by a second set in 1964. The North side cover was completed in 1958 at a cost of £1400, with the terracing under it being finished two years later. In 1980 the cover was extended to run the whole length. A ground record crowd was established in 1967 when 7,200 watched an F.A. Cup match with Reading.

The Pondfield Park terracing was fenced at the rear and the grass banking removed to provide a small training area in the spring of 1991. At this time Redbridge Forest F.C. were sharing the ground in a long-term agreement, and the tenants provided the funds for a new 160 seat stand, turnstiles, tea bar and toilets to be built adjacent to the main stand at the Pondfield Park end. It was just a year later that the two clubs merged to form the current Dagenham & Redbridge F.C.

Left: The Pondfield Park End away terrace.

Below: The Victoria Road terrace 2004.
Bottom: The new Stand 2004.

Dagenham & Redbridge F.C.

The old wooden stand was finally demolished in 2001 and replaced with a new 800-seater in just twelve weeks, opening in time for the Essex Senior Cup Final with Canvey Island on 4th August. During the same year the eight floodlight pylons were removed and replaced with slim corner poles. With improvements still ongoing, the capacity has now reached 6,078 and the ground is of Football League standard. The facilities meet with the approval of their East End neighbours, as West Ham United stage their midweek reserve matches at the ground. *Below: The pitch length covered terrace in 2004. Bottom: The Dagenham & Redbridge stand beyond the new main stand.*

A.F.C. Hornchurch

Hornchurch Stadium,
Bridge Avenue,
Upminster, RM14 2LX

Formed as Upminster Wanderers in 1923, the club moved to Bridge Avenue in 1953. Renamed Hornchurch & Upminster, in 1960 they became Hornchurch F.C. and finally A.F.C. Hornchurch in 2005 after the previous club folded. The first game here was a friendly with Romford on 22nd August and attracted 3,000. In 1954 4,500 watched a benefit match with a West Ham XI. In the early days there was some cinder terracing along the Bridge Avenue side, with benches along the ropes for older supporters.

Below: A view of the record breaking crowd.
Bottom: The first game at Hornchurch Stadium, a 1-1 draw with Romford on 22nd August 1953

The appearance of the ground changed when a 440-yard cinder track was added in 1956. Over the following years a small seated stand was built on the far side, and a terraced cover and small Directors' Stand opposite, but even with the addition of floodlights the feeling was overwhelmingly that this was a spacious athletics track, with a football pitch in the middle.

Above: Hornchurch score against Aveley in the early 1960s. The area where the tea bar on the left of the terrace stood is now fenced off outside the ground.

A.F.C. Hornchurch

In 1989 the club struggled to come to terms with the loss of their clubhouse after a fire, and in 1996 they fought proposals to build houses on the ground.

Above: The temporary uncovered seating installed for the Darlington Cup game in '03.

In 2002 double glazing company Bryco funded redevelopment of the ground, transforming the run-down arena into an 810-seat ground with amenities including a restaurant, bar, gymnasium, toilets on both sides of the ground and three refreshment outlets. A modern version replaced the old wooden officials' stand, and three separate pre-built stands arrived on a lorry. The refurbished main stand then seated 220, and was book-ended by two stands which each housed 150 tip-up seats. A seated area of 250 filled a gap on the near side. The former covered terrace was smartened up.

In 2003 the club reached the 1st Round of the F.A. Cup and their tie with Darlington was live on TV. A temporary uncovered seated stand was erected behind the goal at the clubhouse end. There was little space for standing spectators and a lot of the crowd of 2,186 were shoe-horned into a corner behind the near goal. Victory gave The Urchins a home tie against Tranmere Rovers in Round Two. Temporary covered stands were installed at each end, with red and white striped pitched roofs.

Second top: The Directors Stand, rebuilt in recent years.
Second bottom: The upgraded main stand with a newer addition to the left. A similar cover is hidden away on the right.
Bottom: The covered terrace.

A.F.C. Hornchurch

At around this time the club were thwarted by local residents in their plans to build a large main stand on the Bridge Avenue side. This led to them looking at sites for a possible new home but sadly Bryco went into administration in 2004 at a time when the club were looking a good bet for promotion to the Conference.

After limping through the rest of the season they folded, but were resurrected in 2005/06 as A.F.C. Hornchurch in the Essex Senior League, winning promotion to the Ryman League at the first attempt.

Below: The covered terrace, Directors' Stand & seating area. Bottom: The refurbished original main stand shows the difference between a properly-designed stand and inferior modern versions. Photos: Colin Peel

Ilford F.C.

Cricklefield Stadium,
High Road,
Ilford, IG1 1UE

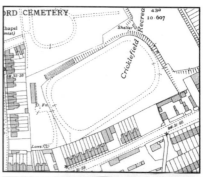

ricklefield has been an athletics ground of note for many years, and the first permanent track on the site of the current one was a five laps to one mile cinder track, which cost £350 and opened on 20th August 1925. It was enlarged to a 440-yard track in July 1933 by cutting a channel through the higher ground to the east of the track. There was once a small dirt/cinder track at that end but it has long since been grassed over. The track was out of use during WWII as the ground was used as a barrage balloon landing base. After the war, the track re-opened on 27th May 1950. During the 1950s and 1960s large crowds gathered to watch the successful Ilford Schoolboys football team play here.

*Top: An OS MAP from 1938. **Above**: The Sir Herbert Dunnico Memorial Gates, formerly at the old Lynn Road ground.*

Ilford F.C.

In 1968 the old Ilford F.C. considered moving here. They had £10,000 debts and offered Redbridge Council £66,000 to improve the stadium, from the overall sum of £100,000 which would have been incoming from the sale of their Lynn Road ground. Another £24,000 would have been deposited with the council. The council were not interested in discussing it, and the outcome for Ilford FC is well known.

The track was altered to 400 metres in the 1970s and upgraded to synthetic in 1987. The official re-opening was on 27th May 1988. At the same time the newly reformed Ilford F.C. were looking to use the ground as their new base for London Spartan League games.

The pitch had been shortened to accommodate the new track, however, and this proved impractical. At the same time Leytonstone & Ilford/Walthamstow Avenue were looking at the venue as a possibility for a new base for their newly merged club.

For a number of years Ilford used various local pitches until they took up residence in 1994 in an intermediate division of the LSL, and continued at the ground in the EBHL. Walthamstow St. Mary's were sharing the ground for their LSL Division 2 games at this time. Ilford gained senior status and were elected to ESL in 1996/97 after the pitch was lengthened, new dressing rooms provided and the 221 seats in the grandstand were re-profiled.

The new cover, erected in just nine days at the end of the 2004/05 season.
Photo: Gavin Ellis

Ilford F.C.

In January 2003 a two-storey club building was opened, aided by a £850,000 National Lottery grant. It houses changing rooms, a kiosk, a boardroom and a first floor bar with sliding doors opening out onto a balcony viewing area. The ground is substantially terraced around but for the far end, and for a track venue the action does not seem too remote. The club were elected to the Southern League for 2004/05, and a required cover for 150 was erected over the far terracing in just nine days at the end of the season. There are two entrances, and at one of them are situated the Sir Herbert Dunnico Memorial Gates, originally at the old Ilford ground in Lynn Road. New for 2005/06 were turnstile blocks both here and at the other entrance on Green Lane. The turnstiles are very old and clearly have a history but the club purchased them from a dealer so their origins are unknown.

Above: The section of terracing to the west of the stand was originally developed before WWII. Below: The sweep of terracing around the east end.

Leyton F.C.

Leyton Stadium,
Lea Bridge Road,
Leyton, E10 7LD

This ground is perhaps better known as The Hare & Hounds, the name deriving from the pub that still stands on Lea Bridge Road. One of the first clubs to play at the ground were Walthamstow Grange F.C. The ground was relatively un-developed at that time and they were eas-ily persuaded to move their 1912-13 F.A. Cup tie with Southend to Roots Hall, al-though the £30 sweetener must have helped! Another occupant was Newportonians F.C., who held senior sta-tus and whose players were former mem-bers of Newport Road Board School in Leyton. They competed in various leagues from their formation in 1895, including the Spartan League between 1908-21, and fi-nally departed the ground in 1919.

Leyton F.C. played at a number of grounds in the area including The Leyton County Ground, Lea Bridge Road and Osborne Road – now the home of Leyton Orient F.C.

After leaving there in 1937 (allowing the then titled Clapton Orient to move across from Lea Bridge Road) they groundshared with Walthamstow Avenue and then Clapton Orient during the WWII, before pitching up for the third time at The Hare & Hounds. They had spent the 1901-05 seasons there, and then 1919-22.

Above: The former cover on the allotment side. Below: The main stand. (Both taken in 1972). Photos: Bob Lilliman
Bottom: An excellent view of the ground in the early 1950's, showing the large terrace in the north east corner.

Leyton F.C.

Large crowds patronised the ground in the post-war boom years, and Leyton went all the way to Wembley in the F.A. Amateur Cup in 1952, losing 2-1 to local rivals Walthamstow Avenue in front of 100,000. Cinder terraces were banked up using wartime rubble, particularly adjacent to the small grandstand, in the North West corner. The stand itself was a small boxy affair, with the

seating deck raised and viewing obstructed by six support columns. It stood behind a wicker fence, with the rest of the pitch fenced off with a solid rail barrier. Surprisingly, the stand survives to this day with two of the columns removed, and glass screen ends added. After allowance for the press and directors' boxes there are only 36 remaining seats for the public. It is likely it wouldn't have lasted past 1955 if a bid for the old wooden stand at Leyton Orient's Brisbane Road (the same ground as the aforementioned Osborne Road) had been successful at that time.

The right-hand end of the ground, from the entrance on the main road, was banked up with cinder terracing but over the years this has been reduced to just a bizarre raised platform inset into the rear garden area of houses in Seymour Road. That not withstanding, plans have been on the table to build a 780-seat stand at that end, utilising seats that were rescued from the old Wembley Stadium in a job lot.

Above: *The three stands on the north side.*
Below: *The new cover on the South side, May 2004. Photos: Colin Peel*

Leyton F.C.

A new cover on the far side was erected a few years ago then extended to run the whole length during 2003/04. It looks neater from the opposite side than it actually is, being a narrow jumble of scaffolding poles and terracing. The centrally-located dugouts seriously restrict the view from this side. At the eastern end there is a pathway, a mesh barrier preventing balls from reaching a stream behind the fence.

Back on the main stand side, two companion covers were added over the years. A small terraced one to the west is partly out of action as it is full of surplus Wembley seats. The other looks older than it actually is, having arrived at some time during the 1980s. It towers over the original stand, is very steep and made from scaffolding and wood. It has seven vertiginous rows and stands partly on the site of the old terracing which was replaced by a car park.

Both ground and club have enjoyed a renaissance in recently after a period which included amalgamation as Leyton-Wingate (1975-92), decampment to Wadham Lodge as Leyton Pennant before the name and history was won back in court! Woodford Town leased the ground in 1996/97 when it was empty and plans for a residential care home were only thwarted by a covenant. Today and a former car showroom on the main road has been replaced with a very impressive blue glass-fronted nightclub which is also the club's new nerve centre. This is a remarkable turnaround for a club that had lost their old clubhouse and changing rooms to a fire in 1976.

Top: The Dagenham Road end.
Middle: The pitch length cover, March 2004.
Bottom: The smallest of the three areas of cover in May 2004. Photo: Colin Peel

Leyton Orient F.C.

Matchroom Stadium,
Brisbane Road,
Leyton, E10 5NF

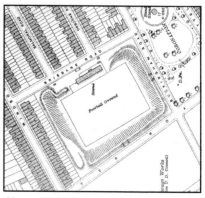

Leyton F.C. were the first team to make the ground their home, settling in for the 1905/06 season at a time when it was better known as Osborne Road. At the time there was a single low 475-seat stand on the east side, referred to as the Orange Box. The rest of ground was made up of embankments, with a cover over the west terrace. The club vacated the ground in 1914 (Bryant & May then used it as their works ground), but returned in 1929 after having reached three successive F.A. Amateur Cup Finals from their Army Sports Ground base (see under St. Vincents F.C.). The council would not renew Leyton's lease on Osborne Road in 1937, at which point Clapton Orient moved in from Lea Bridge Stadium.

Above: 1916 OS Map, at a time when it was the Bryant & May Works Ground.
Below: The full length East Stand and paddock in May 1995.

Photo: Mike Floate

Leyton Orient F.C.

Their first game was a Division Three South match with Cardiff City, attended by a healthy 14,598 although that proved to be above average. The ground was re-named Brisbane Road after WWII, with the host club changing their name to Leyton Orient (and just plain Orient between 1966 and 1987).

*Above: The North end terrace in May 1989. Photo: Colin Peel **Below**: The South Bank terrace in 1994. Photo: Richard Brock*

In the late 1940s the club began to extend the banking around the ground, which over time became concrete terracing with intermittent crush barriers. Each end at the ground had an uncovered terrace and there was a paddock in front of the West Stand.

Photo: Mike Floate

Leyton Orient F.C.

In 1956 the Orange Box was demolished (Leyton F.C. had made a bid to reclaim their old stand) and replaced with a larger stand which had formerly stood at the Mitcham Greyhound Stadium, adjacent to Tooting & Mitcham United's Sandy Lane ground. Initially only two-thirds of the stand were erected, hence the gable is off centre; it was finally completed in 1962. The work was done upon the club's promotion to the old First Division giving a rebuilt west terrace and 3,700 seats in a 35,000 capacity ground. The record gate of 34,345 came in 1963/4 for a local derby with West Ham in the F.A. Cup.

The ground changed little over the years, just seats being fitted over the west terrace and in the former paddock area opposite.

Top: The South E+ast corner, March 2005. Photo: Mike Floate **Above**: The block of flats/offices rises up, October 2005.

Below: The view from the new West Stand. Photo: Leyton Orient F.C.

Leyton Orient F.C.

The arrival of Barry Hearn in 1995 saw plans to turn the pitch through 90 degrees taking in an old sports ground on the west side, and a proposed road realignment. This never happened but the south terrace was bulldozed and a new 1,330-seat stand built, in the Dutch style of having the spectator concourse in a moat below pitch level, and with a bar and catering facilities beneath. Major redevelopment work has since meant that the East Stand has been shortened at each end with four commercial development blocks being built up in each corner. The west terrace has made way for a highly unusual 2,500-seat grandstand with an abnormally high (and pitched!) roof below a single seating tier, a gallery and hospitality boxes. The remaining terrace at the north end has also gone, pending redevelopment. The long term plan is for a 1,500-seat stand to emerge here, similar to the South Stand. Plans have also been approved for a new 4,000-seat East Stand. It has taken a long time, but Brisbane Road is catching up with its Football League contemporaries.

Top: The new South Stand. Photo: Colin Peel Above: The new West Stand starts to take shape. Below: The completed stand. Photos: Leyton Orient F.C.

London APSA F.C.

Terence McMillan Stadium,
Prince Regent Lane,
London E13 8SD

The ground was built as an athletics stadium on the site of a rubbish tip known locally as Beckton Dumps in 1967. The 654 bench seat cantilever grandstand dates back to the first days of the stadium, now part of Newham Leisure Centre. Floodlighting was installed, following the path of the track. Grass banking was built up around the ground and formed vantage points for the record crowd at the ground.

In February 1976 East Ham United 'signed' George Best for one game to play against West Ham in a charity match. Because such a large crowd was expected the game was switched from their inadequate Ferndale Sports Ground to the more spacious McMillan Stadium. A gate of 4,800 saw East Ham lose 7-6. Best scored four and made the other two!

West Ham United Reserves had a short stint there in 1992; Clapton thought briefly of leaving the Old Spotted Dog in 1994. Brazilian FSSC of the MCL spent a few years there, until the end of 2004/05.

Formed in 1993 as Ahle Sunnah F.C., London APSA later made the stadium their home but had to move to Aveley in 2003 to gain senior status. The reserves remained in situ. A year earlier their application to become the first senior Aslan side in Essex was turned down due to the inadequacies of the stadium.

The re-opening finally took place on 4th September 2005, when London APSA entertained Southend Manor (1-2) in front of 51 fans in the ESL. A new pay hut and entrance had been built in Maybury Road but with the narrow pitch in a poor state and the dugouts roofless, it was difficult to determine why it had all taken so long.

Romford F.C.

Ford Sports Club,
Rush Green Road,
Romford, RM7 0LU

Briggs Sports moved here from Victoria Road, Dagenham, in 1955. Owned by the Ford Motor Company, Briggs' reserve team had first used the ground during the 1953/54 season. The club confidently expected 10,000 for the opening game between a Combined Area XI and West Ham on 14th May 1955 but on a cold and rainy day only 5,000 turned up.

The ground had a 600 seat cantilever stand, with glass screen ends flanked on either side by uncovered terracing. For that first game, Briggs Sports' dark green wooden terracing was moved across from Victoria Road and installed at each end. A five step deep pitch-length cinder terrace was in place for the start of the following season. 10,000 fans witnessed the 1957 F.A. Amateur Cup defeat against Bishop Auckland.

Ford United were formed in 1958 from the amalgamation of Ford Sports (1934) and Briggs Sports (1934). For many years the ground changed very little. The wooden terracing at each end didn't last long, and the cinder track declined slowly over the years. Floodlights were the only noticeable improvement (1992) and by 1994/95 Ford were having to play games away from home

as their dressing rooms were said to be a health risk! Unable to obtain the 10-year lease needed to gain promotion to the Isthmian League's Premier Division, Ford left Rush Green in 2001 for Barkingside.

West Ham's youth team then played Academy games here before 2002 when Romford moved in to put their ground problems at Collier Row behind them. The ground today is neatly fenced on all sides, with the track having now disappeared (leaving the pitch a distance from the covered areas), and there is a standing cover opposite over terracing that was concreted during Ford's latter years in residence. Romford had tried to buy Rush Green in 1995/96, when they had entered into a period of groundsharing, prior to the unsuccessful move to Collier Row. If successful Ford would have relocated to Faces F.C.'s current ground at Newbury Park.

Below: *The original grandstand, April 2004.*
Bottom: *A panoramic view before the first game in 1955.*

Romford F.C.

There is an entrance turnstile in each corner at the car park end, further legacies from Ford's Isthmian League days. The main stand now has individual seats in Ford colours of blue and white and a reduced capacity of 345. Somewhat unusually there are two tunnels, one for each side, although for ESL games these are also used by supporters to reach the bar. At this level there are no stewards to prevent supporters standing in front of the stand, although there are enough elevated seats and crowds are sparse enough for this not to be a problem. The cages over the two tunnels block out the view from some of the seats. When the ground first opened it was boasted that every reserved seat ticket holder would have an uninterrupted view of the game!

The owners still refuse to give Romford a 10-year lease and so they continue to look for a new home. Hornchurch's bid to buy the ground floundered in 2004 before they went bust. The long term future for this historic venue does not look good.

Below: The covered terrace.
Bottom: The main stand in August 2003.
Photo: Colin Peel

Sporting Bengal F.C.

and Beaumont Athletic FC
Mile End Stadium,
Rhodeswell Road, E4 7TW

It was at Mile End Green in 1381 that young King Richard II saw off the peasant's revolt, following the fatal wounding of their leader Wat Tyler. The area is quieter these days!

A church once stood on the site now occupied by the stadium, in a park known as King George's Field. It opened in 1967 as King George V Stadium and later became known as East London Stadium. It was reopened with a synthetic athletics track on 9th September 1990 by Sir Arthur Gold of the British Olympic Committee, and renamed Mile End Stadium.

It is now home to West Ham United's Asian Footballers Scheme and Essex/East London's first senior Asian side are based here, although Sporting Bengal F.C. play in the Kent League. Tower Hamlets F.C. began to play at the ground in the LSL in 1986 and continued there for a number of years.

Today the ground is more closely associated with Crown & Manor F.C. who have been there since 1992, playing in the LSL and currently the MCL. In 2003 the throwing cage and shot put circle were removed to increase the pitch size for Sporting Bengal to enter senior football. Over the summer of 2006 it would appear that Beaumont Athletic have replaced Crown and Manor as the second club at the stadium, playing in the ESL.

Photo: Colin Peel

Sporting Bengal F.C.

The record attendance at the ground is not for football but for a concert by Blur on 17th June 1995, with support from 1970s duo Sparks among others. A crowd of 27,000 attended despite poor weather. The grandstand was used as a VIP area on the day, and was packed with celebrities!

The stand is still the focal point of the floodlit ground, although there is a very impressive backdrop away to the right, of Canary Wharf and its accompanying towers. These look particularly impressive when lit up at night.

The Regents Canal runs behind the stand, and an interesting walk can be had along the Thames Towpath down to the Lime-house Basin and beyond. The cantilever roofed stand has 400+ seats reached by two staircases, with a press box at the rear.

On either side of the stand are shallow terraces which stretch around to the corners and then disappear around the bends.

Until 2004 there was a pitch length shallow terrace, four steps deep, on the far side since removed to make way for a swimming pool complex on that side. In a £15m redevelopment an aerobics gym and 5-a-side football courts have also been catered for.

Below: The former shallow terrace on the far side, November 2003.

Thurrock F.C.

Thurrock Hotel,
Ship Lane,
Grays, RM19 1YN

The club was formed in 1985 as Purfleet F.C., starting life as an intermediate club in ESL Div.1. They were connected to Fondu who had previously competed in the EBHL and played on one of two pitches at what had until recently been Aveley Technical College. By the time of the fledgling club's occupation this had become a hotel and today the 52 bedroom Thurrock Hotel towers over the ground on the southern side.

Initially the two pitches ran at right angles to the current one, but the main pitch was turned around during the first season, and then railed. Work then started on the changing rooms, behind which was a WWII bomb shelter (it is still there). Prior to that, the players changed in the hotel and came down a flight of steps which can still be seen next to the club shop. The first pay box was at the top of those steps.

Floodlights went up in January 1988 and were first used for an Essex Thameside Trophy match against Pennant (1-2). The grandstand was next, built in the summer of 1988 to enable the club to accept promotion to the Isthmian League. Its design echoed back a good twenty years with the council insisting it should have a pitched roof. Today it holds 300 yellow and green tip-up seats. Cut into the hillside, a doorway at the back leads directly from the hotel to the Directors' Box.

An aerial view of the ground in 2005. Photo: Thurrock & Basildon College

Thurrock F.C.

Ground improvements have continued, despite the comparative lack of support. In 1992 an 800-capacity covered terrace went up at the Ship Lane end, four years later a neat terraced stand went up at the M25 end, adjacent to the changing block. This was known as The Thurrock & Basildon College Stand until 2005. The remaining side, on the north, was terraced in 1997 and covered in 2005. The M25 end of this stand has been fitted with red tip-up seats, formerly at Cardiff Arms Park, to bring the number up to the required Conference grading. Many clubs purchased seats a little nearer to home, from the old Wembley Stadium. Not Thurrock though....they have part of the pitch! A club member won a competition for some of the Wembley turf and it was re-laid at the ground.

Above: The view from the end terrace to the hotel complex. Photo: Mike Floate
Below: The changing room block. Oct '05.

Below: The main stand. Photo: Mike Floate

Thurrock F.C.

The club has entertained Luton Town and Oldham Athletic in F.A. Cup 1st Round games, but the record attendance of 2,572 was for a friendly with West Ham in 1998. The entrance at the Ship Lane end has eight turnstiles, four in each corner, but only two near the clubhouse open for many games. The clubhouse (opened v Canvey on 3rd March 2001) is to the right, sitting outside the ground. On a match day access is from within the ground. It looks smaller on the inside, due to the large pitched roof and gable. The walls are decorated with photos from their short history and also old framed Purfleet shirts.

Above: The uncovered side terrace, October 2003. *Below*: The terrace complete with roof in October 2005. Photo: Mike Floate

Enough to satisfy most clubs? Not Thurrock! (The name changed in 2004 in a bid to link more successfully locally). When finances allow they intend to build another pitched-roof stand between the main one and the clubhouse, nestling into the old banking. They will be joined together, but with a lower roof on the newcomer. The M25 stand could also go, to make way for a larger replacement and sports facility at that end which would service youth pitches to be developed on adjacent waste ground. Part of finance, it is hoped, would come from Olympic funds if the conveniently located venue gets the thumbs up as a training centre for athletes. The luxury hotel next door certainly gives it an advantage.

Above right: The Ship Lane covered terrace October 2003.
Right: The covered terrace and changing rooms at the M25 end in October 2005. Photo: Mike Floate

Waltham Forest F.C.

Wadham Lodge,
Kitchener Road,
Walthamstow, E17 4JP

View from the South Terrace, 2004.

The ground at Wadham Lodge in Walthamstow has been built up on land recognised as a Sports Ground for many years. Before WWII the current pitch was occupied with tennis courts and there were brick shelters scattered around the rest of the grounds. Pennant F.C. were formed in 1966 and began to play on one of several pitches there. They progressed to the London Spartan League and from a roped off pitch to the current one, which had a small stand erected in 1983 and a permanent rail barrier in 1985. The cover had a disproportionately high roof, given that it was not terraced, and had the lower side panels removed to ease viewing from the back. It was optimistically said to hold 100 but only 30 of those would have had a view of the game! Following the demise of Walthamstow Avenue, the club saw fit to change their name to Walthamstow Pennant in 1988-89.

Floodlights arrived second hand from Leytonstone & Ilford, and were erected in 1989, officially being used first for a local derby with Leyton, watched by a healthy crowd of 860. In 1995 the club agreed to a merger with Leyton and became Leyton Pennant.

Waltham Forest F.C.

Now playing in the Isthmian League, a larger seated stand was built to a similar design and a covered end terrace went up to the left of the entrance, at the north end. A shorter, but uncovered, terrace was built up at the opposite end, finally being covered in 2003 when they again re-branded, this time as Waltham Forest. The fourth side of the ground, opposite the grandstand, is mostly flat standing although there is a small section of uncovered terrace between the dugouts. Here it is four steps deep, but only three at either end. All three terraced areas, though, are interrupted at regular intervals by tubular scaffolding poles. With the many blue support poles at each end (47 in all) these give a very cluttered appearance.

In 1988 this was one of the grounds looked at by Leytonstone & Ilford/Walthamstow Avenue as they looked for a new ground under the name of West Essex United.

A number of Spartan League and Middlesex County League clubs have played on the nearby railed pitch to the left of the Wadham Lodge car park (see entry at rear of book under Hale End Athletic F.C.). Confusingly, amongst those clubs was one called Walthamstow Pennant, between 2003-05! For the 2005-06 season Brazilian FSSC of the MCL are sharing the main pitch and facilities. TV viewers may recognise Wadham Lodge as the training ground of Sky's Harchester United!

Above: An OS Map from 1939; the current ground is where the tennis grounds to the right of the bowling green are.
Below: The South Terrace, 2004.

Below left: The uncovered South Terrace during the Leyton Pennant days in 1996. **_Below right_**: The South Terrace in 2004.

West Ham United F.C.

Boleyn Ground,
Green Street,
Upton Park, E13 9AZ

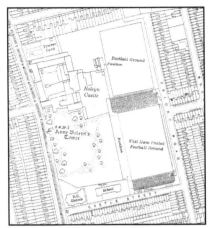

irstly the name of the ground is The Boleyn Ground, and not Upton Park which is the area in which the stadium is located. West Ham United moved here from The Memorial Recreation Ground in 1904. They built a low flat-roofed timber grandstand on the west side, with many obstructing support columns. A pavilion with a covered enclosure lay in the SW corner, used by officials and the press. There was a changing hut in the NW corner; the rest of the ground was cinder banks with wooden barriers. The first game was a local derby with Millwall in The Southern League on 2nd September, watched by 10-12,000. The first stand was replaced in 1913 with a larger construction with changing rooms beneath. The banking was also improved – particularly at the North end – improvements which helped the club gain election to the 2nd Division of the Football League in 1919. At this time there was an additional pitch beyond the North Bank, with its own pavilion adjacent to the halfway line.

Above: An OS map from 1918.

Right: The Chicken Run (upper) replaced an earlier cover on the east side.
Below: Models of the ground by Malavan Models circa 1904 (left) and circa 1962 (right). Photos: Simon Inglis

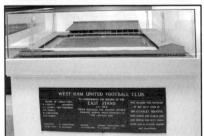

West Ham United F.C.

Success in the 1920s led to yet another West Stand replacement, this time a 1925 double-decker with a pitched roof. This didn't run the whole length of the pitch and fell short of reaching the South end even after an extension in 1965. The roof of West Stand no.2 was salvaged and put up over the terracing on the South Bank. At the same time a small corrugated iron and timber cover was built over the narrow East side, backing on to Priory Street. Complete with wooden terracing, it was reverentially known as the Chicken Run thereafter. The highest attendance to squeeze into the ground was possibly for a Division Two match with Charlton on 18th April 1936. It is said that 43,528 were at the game but this was not substantiated at the time so the club has settled on a figure of 42,322 for the 1970 visit of Tottenham.

There was bomb damage to the South Bank in 1944, which took six years to repair. Floodlights arrived in 1953 with Tottenham the opposition for a friendly fixture. In 1961 the North Bank was covered. Although this was where the more boisterous Hammers fans could be found, the sightlines were appalling and very little could be seen of the near goal. The next development was the sad loss of the Chicken Run in 1968. The new East Stand was up and running a year later, with 3,490 seats and a barrier-free paddock for 3,400. The old name was difficult to shake off though, and the paddock was still lovingly called the chicken run until covered with seats in 1994.

Below: Panoramic views of both ends from the Main Stand in 1992. Photos: Mike Floate

West Ham United F.C.

The South Bank was replaced that year with a fitting tribute to the club's greatest player, the Bobby Moore Stand. This was reminiscent of the larger North Bank Stand at Arsenal, seating 7,592 in two tiers. The following year the Centenary Stand replaced the North Bank. This smaller two-tiered stand seated 5,686, with away supporters usually located on the lower tier. The largest development was completed in 2001 with the opening of the Dr. Martens Stand, the fourth to grace the West side in 100 years. This was opened by the Queen in 2002. Also in two tiers, it wraps around to join up with the two end stands and seats 15,000. From the outside, there is a very impressive façade at the main entrance featuring the two castle turrets from the club badge, themselves a historical nod to the old Boleyn Castle, the last turret of which was knocked down in 1958.

The ground is no stranger to non-League football, in fact for the first 15 years West Ham were a non-League team. In the 1930s five F.A. Amateur Cup Finals were played here, as was the 2003 F.A. Vase Final between Brigg Town and AFC Sudbury, and the 2006 F.A. Trophy Final featuring Grays Athletic and Woking.

Above: *The West Stand in 1995. Photo: Richard Brock* *Below*: *The West Stand, 1925-2000. Photo: Paul Claydon*

Above right: *The East Stand in 1995. Photo: Richard Brock*
Right: *The East Stand in March 1989. Photo: Colin Peel*

West Ham United F.C.

Leyton F.C. once played a home East Anglian Cup game here, but the lowest gate was for a far higher profile fixture. In October 1980 the WHU played Castilla from Spain in a European Cup Winners Cup 2nd Leg tie. There had been crowd trouble in the 1st leg so this match had to be played behind closed doors. The official attendance was nil, but with 262 privileged non-paying spectators in the West Stand. Five hundred policemen ringed the ground to stop anyone trying to get in.

Currently the ground holds 35,647. There were tentative plans to build a new East Stand to increase the capacity to 40,500 but they are on ice until finances stabilise.

Above: The new North Stand. Below: An elevated view of the old East Stand.
Below left: The new Dr. Martens Stand.

The Bobby Moore Stand in 1995. Photo: Richard Brock.

Other Grounds

Arsenal F.C. Youth Academy
Hale End Sports Ground,
99 Wadham Road, Walthamstow.
This was formerly the London Hospital Sports Ground, and backs onto the greyhound stadium at Walthamstow. In the past it was principally used for rugby and had a stand up against the fence along the far boundary. This had six rows of wooden bench seats, a flat roof, end screens, a central support column and a low front wall.

There is a floodlit all-weather facility, opened in July 2001, and an indoor sports hall too. A sign up at the gate just says Hale End Sports Ground, giving little away about the ownership.

The brick two-storey pavilion has the club name – 'Arsenal F.C. Youth Academy' over the lintel and the club badge on the side. There are further pitches to the rear.

Liam Brady describes Hale End as being a mini-version of the Seniors' £10m facility at Shenley, and it was purchased in 1999. The facilities include everything that a star of the future requires: pitches as flat as bowling greens, dressing rooms, showers, physio rooms, a medical room and a canteen.

The old rugby stand can be seen right, on land that now belongs to Arsenal's Youth Academy.

Avondale Rangers F.C.
Dale Park, Buckhurst S&SC,
Roding Lane, Buckhurst Hill.
Rangers play in The Ilford & District League, within sight of Buckhurst Hill F.C.'s home. There is an access bridge to get cars across a stream, a car park and changing rooms behind the goal. These are housed in a graffiti-covered brick building with a metal-shuttered communal room and sheltered area in front of it, (photo below left). On the right side of the ground there is a small building that provides more cover, but no longer faces out onto the pitch since it has been moved further down (photo below right).

Britannia F.C.

Bank of England Sports Ground
(Britannia Club), Langston Road, Loughton.
The host club plays in the Essex Veterans League
and have a very neat set up, visible from the M11
northbound just after J5. There are several pitches,
and the one nearest the entrance (overlapped by a
cricket pitch) has mature trees lining one side and a
grass bank behind the West goal with a large pavil-
ion/social club on top of this. There are two bench
seats behind the goal here, providing the only spectator amenity as such. This venue is very popular with
South Essex clubs during the summer and Barking,
Romford and Barkingside have all hired the ground
out for pre-season friendlies in recent years.

Top: Bench seating on top of the banking.
Above: The Britannia Club buildings.

Brampton Park F.C.

Thames Water, Jenkins Lane, Barking.
Brampton Park of the EBHL play at one of the most
inaccessible grounds in this book. Jenkins Lane once
boasted a floodlit football ground adjacent to the A13
used by Eton Manor among others. It is now partly
covered by a Powerleague clubhouse and all-weather
pitches and will feature in 'The Lost Football Grounds
of Essex and East London'.

Back in the 1990s a football pitch at the southern-
most extremity of the lane was used by Craven F.C.
in The London Spartan League. At the time the
ground was known as the Thames Water Beckton

Sewage Treatment Sports & Social Club. The reformed Ilford club had unsuccessfully tried to move
in there in 1990/91, before going to the Douglas Eyre
Ground in Walthamstow. Before the war the ground
had belonged to Tate & Lyle, but was of less signifi-
cance than their sports ground at Gallions Reach.

Surprisingly the ground still exists beyond the sentry
gate entrance to Thames Water and barbed wire fencing. A pitch-roofed social club runs along the top side
of the ground and there are two breeze-block dugouts on that side, quite some way apart. The ground
is quite tight with no room for a rail or rope surround.

Top: The dug outs during Craven's tenure at the
ground. Photo: Tony Incenzo Above: Emphasising
just how hemmed in the ground is!

Buckhurst Hill F.C.

Roding Lane, Buckhurst Hill.
Buckhurst Hill have developed a fine facility, next door
to the former home of Eton Manor. They have been
at Roding Lane since 1985, with their wooden club
building falling victim to fire in 1999, since when they
have received a £290,000 Football Foundation grant
which enabled them to buy the ground and build a
smart new brick facility (see photo on page 48), with
a clubroom, kitchen, four changing rooms, two for officials, full wheelchair access and a raised viewing
area alongside the main pitch.

The club runs 20 teams from the site. The clubhouse
is called the Sherrin Richbell Clubhouse, after Chairman Ken Richbell and President Ray Sherrin.

Buckhurst Hill F.C.

There are two pitches on the main ground. Since leaving the Essex Business Houses League in 2004, the pitch has been roped off for Herts County League fixtures. Previously, the adjacent pitch had often been used for first team games.

Canning Town F.C.
Goosley Playing Fields, East Ham.
The club started in 1948 as Co-ordinated Traffic Services, becoming Co-ordinated Traffic in the early 1950s. Home matches were played at Prince Regent Lane. They then ground-shared for many years with Clapton F.C. at the Old Spotted Dog. As they continued to move around the East End they played at Lyle Park, Bradfield Road, Silvertown in the 1960s, into the 1980s they were at Kennard Street Community Centre, and then Southern Road in the mid-90s.

At the start of 2003/04 they had some ground problems, and Frenford Senior came to their aid with the offer of a pitch to play on. Their current ground is a basic playing field with a small changing block that has no windows. Their pitch is roped off for EOL fixtures, although there are no dugouts.

The club train at the new West Ham United community pitch at Albatross Close in Beckton and are looking to play first and second team games there in future (see page 70). Home first team EOL games for 2005/06 were played at the Terence McMillan Stadium, home of London APSA F.C.

Coopers Metrostars F.C.
The Coopers Company and Coborn School, St. Mary's Lane, Upminster.
The resident club is a Sunday League team, formed in 2003. The main school pitch has a new pavilion behind the goal at the school end, with a raised covered viewing area on the first floor (below).

Crowmill F.C.
Barkingside Recreation Ground, Mossford Green, Redbridge.
While Sunday Leaguers Crowmill do not justify inclusion here, it should be noted that between 1932 and 1957 their current ground at Barkingside Recreation Ground was used by Barkingside F.C. The 25-year period, interrupted by WWII, saw them compete in the Ilford & District, South Essex, Walthamstow, Amateur Football Alliance and London Leagues. The ground was shared with the local cricket club, but they had separate HQs. The original wooden football club changing rooms remain (photo below), complete with a covered section in front, and there is a shuttered refreshment kiosk on the left. There was never a grandstand at the ground, which still has room for two pitches, one either side of the cricket square. Old Parkonians F.C. played here too, in the Southern Amateur League, between 1926-88. They were unable to gain a place in the top division of that league until after Ipswich Town had left for the Eastern Counties League in 1935. Another familiar name to have played here were Frenford Senior during WWII.

Debden Sports F.C.

Debden Sports Club, Chigwell Lane, Loughton.
The club was formed in 1946 and brought in old army huts for use as changing facilities and headquarters. Sixty years on these are still in use! At one time the ground was known as Debden & LCC Sports Ground. The ground is very close to Debden tube station, although the ground has a surprisingly rural feel given the quick rail link to the centre of London and also the M11 which thunders by the far touchline. Passing through the R.J. Williamson Memorial Gates there is a small car park and the old club buildings. The club bar is housed in a green pitched roof timber hut and within there are numerous old team pictures on the wall and other souvenirs including a signed Barcelona shirt. There are two pitches within the immediate complex, although the top one is used less than one in the meadow at the far end. The main pitch is at the bottom of the field, and is neatly roped off. There are no dugouts. Behind the near end goal is a small floodlit training area, with two full size goals and interesting lighting pylons. At the 2006 EOL AGM, the club was voted out of the league.

Faces F.C.

Ford Sports & Social Club, Newbury Park.
This ambitious club has Essex Senior League aspirations, but sadly not a ground to match. That said, this second Ford-owned sports ground in Essex is an attractive venue. There are three cricket pitches here, five football pitches and a rugby pitch. Faces F.C. is the highest ranked club at the venue, although it is also home to BRSA and Port of London Authority of the Essex Business Houses League. The latter club once had its own, very impressive, ground in Ilford but nowadays fields only a Veterans side. Faces have a significant association with the South Essex nightclub chain, which can be found in Ilford, Gants Hill, Basildon and Hoddesdon. The main pitch is alongside the luxurious social club but because of cricket, which overlaps the main pitch, early and late season games are played on outer pitches. When in use, the

main pitch is partly surrounded by a blue metal railing and also a double section of blue rope. Dugouts are available, but are not moved into position for every first team game.

Ford Inter-Departmental League Pitch

Ford Sports & Social Club, Rush Green, Romford.
Visitors to Romford F.C.'s ground at Rush Green will be familiar with the presence of a floodlit grass pitch to the left of the main arena. This is not enclosed and has no covered accommodation, dugouts or rope surround. Three floodlight poles line each side of the pitch, with two standard lamps on each. One might expect either EBHL clubs Sungate or Toby to use this

pitch, as in the past they have been the highest ranked Saturday teams to play on the various other grass pitches here. However, the facility is used sparingly for the exclusive use by the Ford Inter-Departmental League and is kept in an excellent condition.

Frenford Senior F.C.

Oakfield Sports Ground, Forest Road, Barkingside.
The Frenford club were founded in 1928 and have played at a number of grounds in South Essex, including Barkingside Recreation Ground and Goodmayes Park Extension, Goodmayes Lane, Ilford. A facility is still maintained adjacent to Ilford F.C.'s Cricklefield home.

Locating the ground can be confusing in an area with such a proliferation of sports grounds and pitches. One of the entrances to the Oakfield Sports Ground is through the car park of the Redbridge Sports Centre, next to Fairlop tube station. A narrow drive passes beside the ground of Old Parkonians F.C. and into the large car park next to the Jack Carter Pavilion. Old Parks themselves, just to keep things straight forward, played at Oakfield between 1988-93.

The superb pavilion was opened on 3rd June 1998 by HRH Duke of Edinburgh, the Patron of the London Federation of Clubs for Young People, marking the club's 70th anniversary. It was named after the founder of the club, Jack Carter (1907-1995). A memorial cupola clock was added to the pavilion in 1999. A covered area looks out over the cricket ground, but the football pitch is to the left of this. It is one of a handful of EOL grounds to be fully railed off.

On the near side there are gaps between the rails for two new and sturdy dugouts, built in 2006, and heavily secured on non-matchdays. There are further gaps behind each goal as the pegged goal-netting extends beyond the barrier. On the far side of the pitch a red and white plastic banner is displayed on matchdays proclaiming a warm 'Welcome to Frenford Senior FC'. It is accompanied by several other adverts.

Hackney Marshes

Hackney Marshes, Hackney, London.
For over 50 years Hackney Marshes has been the 'home' of grass-roots football in the U.K. and possibly even the world. The 72 full-size pitches (109 as recently as 1992) are certainly the largest concentration found anywhere in Europe. Every weekend over 100 matches take place here involving adults, women and children. The pitches are so tightly packed together that touchlines run within a yard of each other and matches are frequently interrupted by the retrieval of balls from neighbouring pitches. For a team to be able to locate their allotted pitch in time for kick-off is an acquired skill.

Before WWII the low lying Marshes would frequently flood. To the South West they were bordered by the Hackney Cut Navigation Canal and to the North East by the River Lea and Waterworks River, which passed either side of the East Marsh. There was a pavilion on the Marshes and football was played there, but it was only after WWII that it developed to the extent it is famous for today. The marshes were built up using rubble from East End air-raids to prevent flooding, and four islands on the River Lea were joined to the land by infill, while the first stretch of Waterworks River, by the East Marsh, was also filled in. Today, the boundary line separating the London Boroughs of Hackney and Waltham Forest still follows the path of the former rivers, deviating around a non-existent island to the north, and along the former path of the river to the East.

Over the years that have followed many famous names have graced Hackney Marshes, including Terry Venables, Bobby Moore, David Beckham and Sol Campbell. To some the innovation of goal-nets was not discovered until graduating to playing on other grounds!

In 1997 Nike filmed an advert on the Marshes, entitled 'Parklife' and utilising the Blur track of that name. It featured Eric Cantona, Ian Wright, David Seaman, Robbie Fowler, David Batty and Steve Stone in a glorious fuel packed celebration of football at its finest.

Two years later the grounds were the obvious choice as the venue for the first 'Official UK 5-a-Side Football Championships'. Hundreds of teams from all over England gathered over three days to take part in the competition which featured adult, women and youth tournaments and celebrities, including Rio Ferdinand and Frank Lampard. The problem of playing so many five-a-side games outdoors was overcome by building 103 separate pitches – one for each qualifying group and a world record, it was claimed. Each was surrounded by a four foot-high wall full of adverts from companies keen to be seen to endorse an initiative backed by the Prime Minister, Tony Blair. The main attraction on the day was the astonishing sight of a 3,000 capacity all-seater stadium which had been erected specially for the occasion. This comprised of four sides of uncovered seating around a pitch which was larger than all the others. On the top of one side was the TV camera gantry for Sky, who broadcast live coverage. A giant screen on the opposite side relayed live match action. I had accepted an offer to give up my Sunday to play in this tournament, my first match on the Marshes for 26 years, without really appreciating what I was heading for. Unfortunately my camera stayed at home on this occasion.

There were even a dozen or so turnstiles to ensure that all spectators coughed up £5 for entrance and a glossy colour programme. There was a fun fair and many other types of amusements as well as, naturally, dozens of fast food outlets and sizeable beer tents. On an extremely hot day, the stadium was sadly under-utilised and was largely empty even for the celebrity fixtures.

The problem with events of this nature is that players tend to head for home (via that beer tent) after being eliminated rather than sticking around for the final. Nine players were subsequently snapped up by league clubs having been spotted in this tournament. The event returned to Hackney for each of the next three years but was down sized and took place on the smaller East Marsh. The adult teams upholding the finest traditions of grassroots football on the Marshes during the 2005/06 season included 35 clubs from the Hackney & District League. Only 8 of its member clubs play elsewhere – and they are all down the road at Victoria Park!

Top: Some of the 103 individual 5-a-side pitches laid out in 1999 – a world record. Photo: Tom Miller

Below and left: *Evocative photos of Hackney Marshes by Gavin Ellis*

Hackney Marshes – East Marsh

Ruckholt Road, Hackney, London.
The Official UK 5-a-Side Championships returned to Hackney in 2000 but was played on the East Marsh. Fewer teams competed and the focal point stadium has been reduced to less than 2,500 seats. These were still arranged on all four sides of the ground, in rows of green uncovered seats nine deep.

There were further UK Championships on the East Marsh in 2001 and 2002. The stadium for the latter year did not extend beyond three full sides and there was the somewhat surreal sight of operatic legend Pavarotti hovering over the ground in full regalia, in a hot air balloon! The event downsized again in 2003 when it moved to the Powerleague Sports Ground in Forest Road, Hainault (see under Westhamians F.C.) and it did not take place at all in 2004.

In 2000 plans were announced for a major sports facility on the East Marsh, including a separate 400 metre running track and a terraced football stadium adjacent to Ruckholt Road. Nothing materialised.

On 22nd May 2004 a Middlesex County League Division 1 match was played on the East Marsh. Bethnal Green United had lost the use of Victoria Park to cricket, so hired out the ground for their fixture with Harefield Ex-Services, which they won 3-0.

With the success of the London 2012 Olympic bid, the East Marsh has again been in the news. It has been identified as a coach park due to its accessibility from major arterial routes. Much of the East Marsh would be concreted over, and the promises to put it back to its original form afterwards have not impressed the environmentalists who are keen to emphasise that the rare 110-year old native black poplar trees can not be replaced. The old pavilion with its clock is also lined up for bulldozing treatment.

*Top: The old pavilion. **Above**: The temporary stadium and big screen in 2002.*
***Below**: Part of the crowd during the 2002 Official UK 5-a-Side Championships.*
***Bottom**: Bizarrely, that's Pavarotti in the hot air balloon! Really! Photos: Tom Miller*

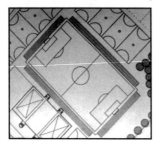

***Left**: Abandoned plans for a stadium on the East Marsh, 2000.*

Hale End Athletic F.C.
Wadham Lodge, Kitchener Road, Walthamstow.
Formed in 1928, Hale End formerly had a close association with their neighbours Walthamstow Avenue. They play in the Premier Division of the Amateur Football Combination on a railed-off pitch to the left of the car park at Waltham Forest's ground. There is no hard standing around the pitch, and portable wooden dug outs are carried into position for each game. Two training lights rest on the rail behind the near goal, illuminating a grass court. The teams change in the block used by Waltham Forest and there is a small amount of distant overhang cover there for the wettest of days, not that Hale End attendances often reach double figures. There are two further pitches, but these are not railed.

In the past a number of clubs have used the pitch in the old London Spartan League, including Leyton County, Clapton Villa and Singh Sabha in the mid 1990s. More recently a revived Walthamstow Pennant club shared the pitch between 2003-05 for its Middlesex County League fixtures. There were rumours that they would merge with Kent League side Sporting Bengal United but instead they threw in their lot with Walthamstow Avenue 2000 and moved out to Town Mead in Waltham Abbey.

Harold Wood Athletic F.C.
Harold Wood Recreation Ground,
Harold View, Harold Wood.
The park within which the club plays was originally bequeathed to the community by the Matthews family for recreational use. The club have played there ever since formation in 1907, wearing claret and blue in homage to West Ham United, whom most of the original team supported. The cricket club joined them in the park when an additional field was donated for their exclusive use by Edward Bryant in 1934. The football club's old wooden changing room structure was destroyed by fire in the 1960s and was replaced by a brick pitched roof building that faced on to the cricket square. Latterly there was a sign on the frontage that declared it to be the headquarters of 'Harold Wood Cricket and Football Clubs'. There were training lights on the roof for the footballers to take advantage of in the winter months.

Several pitches within the spacious park have been used. For a number of years the bumpy pitch that runs alongside the driveway from the main entrance to the car park was considered to be their home, and this had two metal park benches up against a brick wall at the top end. During the 2004-05 season they were using a pitch at right angles to this, on the other side of a line of trees. This was further from the changing facilities but of better quality and being tree lined on three sides still had a closed in feel to it. Weeping Willow trees all but engulfed the near end goal, and so this end was the only one not to be roped off.

Disaster struck the club on the evening of 28th October 2005. A stolen vehicle was burnt out next to the club house, the building was gutted and the club lost its entire memorabilia collection. Despite this set-back the club used alternative changing facilities in the park and won the 2005/06 Essex Olympian League.

Below: The touchline on the pitch currently in use
Bottom: The pavilion, 6 months before the fire

Heath Park F.C.

Aveley Sports & Social Club, Purfleet Road, Aveley.
This ground was formerly the home of Thames Mills F.C. and has previously gone under that name as well as Thames Board Mills and more recently the London Fire Brigade Welfare Ground. It is currently Aveley Sports & Social Club.

East Thurrock United were here for two seasons between 1982 – November 83 in the ESL, being forced to leave after the New Thames Club failed to pay their rates and were put into liquidation. Pitches were borrowed for the rest of the season and one home game was even played 45 miles away at Coggeshall Town.

The ground is a large sports field with an enormous and decorative pavilion that ran alongside part of the pitch that the club used. There was no permanent barrier around the pitch and this was a major problem to the ESL. In 2005/06 Heath Park F.C. played its EBHL First Division fixtures here.

Leyton Orient F.C. Under-16s

Low Hall Farm Sports Ground,
South Access Road, Walthamstow.
There are many grass pitches at Low Hall. The main ground is a former banked cinder track, which had been developed before WWII, at a time when a tramway angled away from South Access Road (then known as Essex Road). Today a pitched-roof clubhouse stands along one side and the track – used by Walthamstow A.C. until the 1970s - has been grassed over. This has left room for two pitches in the middle, positioned widthways.

Chingford moved their Spartan League games here during 1997/98 when there was a fire at Newgate Street and they had lost their clubhouse and dressing rooms. Today several Ilford & District League clubs play here, including Leyton All Stars, Renegades, Woodberry Downs and Warriors. The most prominent user is currently Leyton Orient's under-16 side.

On Wednesday 24th May 2006 Middlesex County League side Brazilian FSSC hired out a pitch for their league match with Walthamstow Avenue & Pennant, as their Wadham Lodge ground was unavailable.

Above: Mature trees top the banks at the Low Hall Farm Sports Ground, creating a delightfully rural feel.

Below: This OS map from 1936 shows the Low Hall Farm Sports Ground, with a tramway seen turning away to the north east from the road.

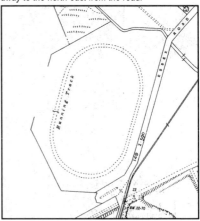

Leyton Orient F.C. Youth & Ladies

Ive Farm Sports Ground, Ive Farm Lane, Leyton.
A short walk from Leyton Orient's ground lies the historic Ive Farm sporting venue. This ground was once a cricket ground of some note. As far back as 1926 a cinder track separated the pitch from four deep steps of cinder terracing that ran along the banking on three sides of the ground.

Later, athletics would take greater prominence, as indicated by the reconfigured 440 yard cinder track and sweeping expanses of grass banking at either end, with concrete walls cut into each one. A large expanse of the banking was cut away in the 1960s to access the land beyond it, with adjacent wartime allotments then being transformed into an additional sports field.

The ground was used by Walthamstow Trojans in the London Spartan League. They spent more than a decade here until that league amalgamated with the South Midlands League in 1997. Classic Inter spent a shorter spell here as a London Spartan League Division 2 side, in the mid 1990s. At that time there was a white 1950s monolithic pavilion structure along the North side of the track, separated from it by a pitch length railing. The central section had a small area of standing cover and there were up to 15 benches in front of the pavilion and along the touchline. On the far side the end banking tapered away to leave a lengthy flat area which gave access to a second pitch around the back.

Perhaps the best opportunity to develop the ground was lost when the London F.A. turned down the Trojans bid for senior status in 1987. In 2001 plans were implemented to knock down the old pavilion and replace it with a 'Football in the Community' centre. With the smart blue pitch roofed changing block finally in place, Leyton Orient Ladies moved in to Ive Farm from the Peter May Sports Centre, Walthamstow, on 5th December 2004, beating Gillingham 2-1 in the Greater London League.

There is no longer a barrier around any part of the pitch so for these games a red and white tape is stretched along much of the inside of the track on the pavilion side, keeping spectators at bay. There are also portable dugouts on that side. In 2005 Leyton Orient returned to use the ground as a training base and also for under-18 matches.

Above: The formerly cinder terraced banking at the west end.

Below: The functional but austere lines of the former pavilion building, now demolished.

Above: Red and white tape forms a token attempt to hold the crowd back before a ladies match.

Below: The recently built modest replacement pavilion.

Leytonstone United F.C.

Ilford Wanderers RUFC, Forest Road, Hainault.
The saving grace of this EOL venue is an interesting dormer-windowed pavilion, overlooking the grass pitches of Ilford Wanderers RUFC and Leytonstone United FC. The wood panelling and historical rugby artefacts and shirts within the dark walls are well worth seeing. The pitches are separated by a cricket square, but neither have any permanent features at the ground. There are however training lights behind the goal. On match days the football pitch is roped off but there are no dug outs. The players change in an annexe to the main pavilion and this is cleverly joined to the main building by a wooden wall, making it appear to be all one building. The pavilion is a pre-war structure and was previously owned by Lloyds Sports Club. Ilford Wanderers RUFC moved in as recently as 1980. Formed in 1947, Leytonstone United are enjoying a relative period of stability at the venue. They once rented a pitch at New Wanstead Flats, spent a single season at Marsh Lane, Leyton and in 1975 arranged a groundshare at Leytonstone FC's former Granleigh Road home. Like all of the other grounds in Forest Road, whether this ground is actually in Hainault or Barkingside depends on who you speak to and what you read!

London & Essex F.C.

Hainault Recreation Ground, Forest Road, Hainault.
As Hainault Playing Fields this sports ground was home to Barkingside between 1929-32. Part of the huge expanse of pitches stretching from Barkingside and Fairlop through to Hainault, it is the largest of the grounds with 14 full size pitches. London & Essex F.C. of the IDL are among the Saturday clubs who play here, as do Durning and Melbourne Sports Reserves of the same league. The monolithic two-storey pavilion (photo above right) is on its last legs and dates back to Barkingside F.C.'s occupation.

Loughton F.C.

Avondale Close, Loughton.
The club purchased the ground in 1990 - details of their former home appears later in the book. Initially only the youth teams played here as the pavilion was not completed until 1993. The club optimistically advised that they would play at Avondale Close in the London Spartan League for 1993/94, but the pavilion would not have been finished in time and they would have had to play elsewhere – if they hadn't folded. When reformed in 1998 the men's team finally got to play competitively here and in 2003 they were accepted into the Herts County League.

The ground is discreetly tucked away at the end of Avondale Close where a sign at the entrance to a small car park announces the name of the host club. The pavilion was constructed by cobbling ten portakabins together and houses four changing rooms to accommodate the two pitches. Only the two used by the first team and their opponents have showers. There is also a lounge with kitchen and servery, which sells hot and cold food and drinks and also club souvenirs. The building is painted in red & black and is showing its age, as do most constructions of this type. There is a railed viewing platform in front, set back from the pitch but not so far that there isn't a good view.

The club initially created a small railed area on the side nearer the clubhouse, perhaps as small as one-fifth of the pitch length. Concerted efforts were made during 2006 to extend this around the rest of the ground. A second, junior, pitch runs lengthways to the right behind the goal. This club are completely unconnected to Loughton Athletic, who played briefly in the ESL in the mid 1980s.

Another club, Loughton Town played at River Playing Fields at Greenstead Road in the 1960s, behind the current clubhouse building.

Photos above: Loughton FC

Right: The M&B Club FC clubhouse
Below: The turnstile at M&B Club FC

M & B Club F.C.
May & Baker Sports & Social Club,
Dagenham Road, Dagenham.

This large Sports Ground is up a long drive way beyond Aventis signboards. The name of the ground currently depends on what you read and who you speak to. The car park is huge and is just beyond a full size pitch which is roped off with metal stakes and which has wooden portable dugout frames. Inventively, these are designed to fit over standard park benches!

M & B Club played in the EBHL until 2006, when they were elected to the EOL. The main pitch is beyond the smart pavilion/clubhouse building, shoe-horned into an area where it is hemmed in on two and a half sides by a line of conifers and the perimeter fencing. It is also partially roped-off with a couple of park benches along the touchline. In one corner there is an ID-activated electronic turnstile through which employees pass between the adjacent factory and the sports ground.

At one time the club played at the rear of the factory backing onto the railway line, as did Toby F.C. There was no stand as such but there was a covered area with seats on a verandah in front of the pavilion. This became part of a drum store, and then partly a lake in the late 1970s.

Below: The social club and dressing room block at Manford FC; the old stand area was to the right

Manford Way F.C.

London Marathon Sports Ground,
Forest Road, Hainault.

This club was founded in 1946 as Hainault Labour Club, changing name to Manford Way a year later. The origins of the name lie around the road of the same name in Chigwell Village. Early games were played there before moving out in 1989 and on to a ground at Fairlop which had been home to the Old Blues Rugby Club from 1922 to 1982. The Old Blues were former scholars from Christ's Hospital, a school based in Horsham, West Sussex. The ground then passed into the hands of the London Postal Regions Sports Club and for a number of years was used by Post Office football and cricket teams.

Above: The Old Blues RUFC grandstand

An elevated grandstand was built during the rugby club's post-war tenure, its high roof stretching out past the adjacent two storey clubhouse (photo p. 57). Although the exact construction date is not to hand, it is known to have been built prior to 1962. The seating deck of six to eight rows of bench seats was reached by a single side staircase. In its latter years it was considered to be unsafe and was strictly out of bounds on a match day. The cost of adding a second staircase to ease evacuation concerns was too prohibitive to entertain, making the eventual demolition in the early years of the new millennium inevitable.

Manford Way have prospered since gaining intermediate status in 1999 and the main pitch now has a permanent white railing around it. In 2000 The London Marathon Charitable Trust purchased the ground on behalf of the London Playing Fields Society, a most agreeable deal where the Trust provides the capital and underwrites the operating losses!

On match days smart Perspex dugouts are lifted into place in front of the site of the old stand. The clubhouse building has a bar and function room which both overlook the pitch. While still some way short of senior status, Manford Way would seem to be one of the clubs more likely to be able to move up in the future.

Romford F.C. were looking at the possibility of developing a new home here, but their plans never got off the drawing board. In the late 1990s their Under-18s staged EJA games here. Potters Bar Town have allowed their Under-18s to travel many miles to the ground to fulfil their EJA fixtures.

Metpol Chigwell F.C.

Metropolitan Police Sports Club, High Road, Chigwell.

The Metropolitan Police Sports Club is housed at Chigwell Hall, which was built in 1876 as a country home. It is a Grade II listed building and was commissioned by Alfred Savill, the founder of Savill's Estate Agency, and built by Norman Shaw. Alfred's brother Walter had a joint enterprise with Norman Shaw which is still known as the Shaw Savill Shipping Line. After Savill died in 1905, Chigwell Hall was purchased by Mr. Walter Waugh and remained in his family until 1938, when it was purchased by the Metropolitan Police.

It is situated on the High Road, Chigwell, just South of the junction with Roding Lane. A true Sports Ground, with a number of football and cricket pitches, bowling green, putting green, assault course facilities, squash, tennis and even a miniature train line. Within the grounds there is even an old mounted police station dating back to 1780!

Below: This cover once stood on the far side but has since been moved nearer the main cricket pitch

Above: Uncovered bench seating by the main pitch.
Right: A small cover and dugout on one of the outer pitches, hidden behind a hedge

Chigwell Police F.C. were founded in 1978 as Three District (M.P.) F.C. In 1980 they became Three Area (M.P.) F.C. When they joined the Spartan League in 1986 they became Chigwell Police and adopted the current name in the early 1990s. They were originally formed to bridge a gap between Police Tuesday and Thursday sides and the Metropolitan Police F.C. team. At the end of the 1986/87 season the club should have been relegated to the Intermediate Division, but member clubs voted to keep them in Division 1. They were unable to gain senior status because of the distance of the changing rooms, some 60 yards from the pitch.

At this time the first team, as now, played on a roped off pitch behind the hall. There were seven rows of uncovered bench seating (catering for over 400) on one side of the pitch and at the bottom of a steep slope on the other were two small covered enclosures which held about 15 spectators each. Over the years these covers have been moved to elsewhere on the 42 acre site. One cover is opposite the main cricket square within sight of the seated area. The other is now on a separate pitch hidden far away to the right, beyond the furthest reaches of the miniature railway line, which terminates at Hylands Junction near one corner flag. The hidden pitch also has dug outs.

Back at the main pitch, there is now a solitary dugout on the far side. To the left and lying at right angles is another pitch which also has dugouts. The excellent facilities are very popular with clubs during the preseason period when their own pitches are being reseeded. The Surrey based Metropolitan Police side and Ilford and Romford are all frequent users, as have been Aveley and Eton Manor Reserves in 2004/05. The latter club even looked into developing their own senior ground here.

Millwall Albion F.C.

Millwall Park, Manchester Road, Millwall.
It might not look like it today, but this park was once a Southern League ground, playing host to Millwall Athletic (now just plain Millwall of the Football League) between 1902-10. The ground was known at the time as the North Greenwich Ground and replaced an earlier ground at nearby East Ferry Road (featured in the 'Lost Football Grounds of Essex & East London' book). In a short space of time a field was prepared with a 500-seat stand on the South side. A narrow stretch of uncovered seating ran for most of the opposite side, with the Globe Rope Works situated just behind.

Banking was developed at the western end from earth excavated when levelling the pitch, and subsequently terraced. The Millwall Extension Railway ran behind this goal, intersecting the South West corner with the turnstiles accessed by going under the viaduct arch opposite House Street. Additional terracing was provided by moving bleachers across from Poplar Park where they had been used in conjunction with Queen Victoria's Jubilee celebrations.

Millwall's opening match here was a friendly with Aston Villa (2-0) on 18th September 1902. Attendances were variable; at the top end 15,000 crammed into the ground for the local derby with West Ham in 1910, but this was exceptional and ultimately the club chose to relocate to New Cross, South of the river, where they anticipated crowds would grow.

The ground lay derelict for many years, but eventually reverted to parkland. The terracing at the railway end became overgrown with time and amazingly the banking still exists despite having recently been landscaped.

The railway itself got a second lease of life when the track bed was used for the Docklands Light Railway and Mudchute Station is now next door. Football has continued to be played at the park, as have rugby and cricket. In 2004 a Football Foundation grant of £302,000 contributed toward the cost of six changing rooms and three referee's rooms, all far grander than the sheds used in the Southern League days. Most of the football played at the venue these days is youth/school related although Millwall Albion of the EBHL were pleased to call it home. Unfortunately, they were unable to fulfil their fixtures in 2005/06 and resigned from the league.

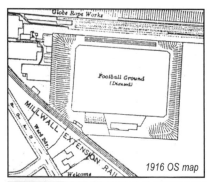

1916 OS map

Top & above: *Millwall attack the Preston NE goal in an FA Cup tie at North Greenwich in 1902/3.*

Above & below: *Versus Bristol R. in an earlier round.*

Above: *Millwall Park in 2006 looking towards the old end terrace.* **Below**: *The turnstiles arch; the stand in the photos left stood on the far side in front of the old Rope Works embankment. Pics: Mike Floate*

Mountnessing F.C.

Hendersons Sports & Social Club, Kenilworth Avenue, Harold Park, Romford.

Despite a picturesque sporting facility adjacent to Mountnessing Windmill, the club is unable to find a ground up to Essex Olympian League standard in its own village. They had been using The Drive, Warley (currently used by Shenfield F.C.) until the former home of Sporting Club Henderson became available. That team still operate a Veterans team from this venue. For 1995/96 they had changed their name briefly to Harold Hill F.C., but then pulled out of the EOL at the end of the season. Perched on a hill on the very edge of Romford, very close to the M25, is this homely facility. There are two pitches, separated by a cricket pitch and a rustic, weather-boarded pavilion with an overhang that fails to provide any relief from the elements. Given the choice, the first team prefer to use the pitch nearest the entrance and rope it off on match days. Of slight interest to the anoraks reading this are the unusual thin corner flags which are black and white in alternate one foot lengths. There are three picnic tables outside the pavilion, which houses a small bar.

Old Buckwellians F.C.

Guru Gobind Singh Khalsa College,
Roding Lane, Chigwell.

Old Buckwellians are the old boys team for Buckhurst Hill County High School, and were formed in 1949. The school closed in 1989 but the football team survives in the Amateur Football Combination. To ensure a continued supply line of players, the club now accepts former pupils of the Roding Valley High School too.

The old school building itself is now known as Guru Gobind Singh Khalsa College, and the first team continues to play on a pitch in front of this very impressive building.

The old pavilion sits behind the second pitch. Below: The main pitch alongside the imposing college buildings.

A tatty old blue board at the entrance announces the club by name. There is a little-used gabled pavilion behind the goal furthest from the road, with an area of cover beneath its extended roof. There is a second pitch here, nearer the M11 which roars past out of sight. The club uses the facilities of Loughton Cricket Club for hospitality purposes, just down the road opposite Buckhurst Hill F.C.

Old Chigwellians F.C.

Roding Lane, Chigwell.

The club is for the old boys of Chigwell School and was formed in 1924. Before WWII they played at a ground near what is now Debden Station. In 1946 they started to play at Buckhurst Hill C.C.'s second eleven ground next to the River Roding and stayed there until 1980 when the society purchased the current grounds and clubhouse in Roding Lane, Chigwell. This is a modern building, with an attractive bar area overlooking the main pitches and a number of changing rooms.

In the nearest field there are two pitches. The top one, nearest the clubhouse is a little flatter than the one next to it, and half way along one touchline there are four wide steps leading up to some grass hockey pitches. Beyond the second pitch is a training area, with its own primitive lighting poles. In the field beyond the end-hedgerows there is a large field which contains four more pitches and a cricket pitch. One of these pitches has four benches alongside it.

The next pitch along has an ornate pavilion behind one goal – clearly pre-dating their arrival at the ground - and a cricket scoreboard behind the other. There are other pitches in fields as far as the eye can see. Currently competing in the Arthurian League, there is no need to rope the pitches off and there are no dugouts either.

Right: An OS map of Blake Hall in 1939, when it was home to Green & Silley Wier.
Below: Old Esthameians FC

Old Esthameians F.C.
Blake Hall Sports Ground,
Blake Hall Road, Wanstead.
This sports ground is one of many that his been used by a number of clubs over the years. Green & Silley Weir were here before WWII and into the 1960s. The works team of the famous ship repairers, the parent company employed thousands of people in Blackwall, Millwall, Royal Albert Dock and Tilbury (where they also had a sports ground in Church Road).

After WWI the football team held senior status, and competed in the F.A. Cup in 1920/21. The company itself was incorporated into River Thames Ship Repairers in 1977 and closed in 1980.

The facilities were once considered sufficient for West Ham United to train here. There are several grass pitches, with the main pitch being on the far side. This is now used by Old Esthameians F.C. (formed 1919) of the Southern Amateur League and there are two concrete dugouts alongside this pitch but no other spectator amenities and the pitch is not currently roped off for games. There is a large pre-war mock-tudor pavilion sitting back behind a long and narrow car park. This incorporates a bar and several changing rooms.

Old Esthameians formerly played at Langdon School in East Ham (see Newham United) and the wide open spaces of Wanstead Flats. Wanstead Town joined the Essex Intermediate League in 1999, playing here. In 2003 they merged with Ryan F.C. under that club's banner and moved to their ground in Chingford. In the past the facilities have been hired out by senior clubs for pre-season friendlies.

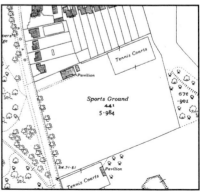

Old Foresters F.C.

The Park, Forest School,
College Place, Snaresbrook.
Forest School was founded in 1834 and is the only major independent school in London's East End. It has a tradition of excellence in sport, music and drama as well as 30 acres of playing fields in Epping Forest. The original Forest club (1859) played at Snaresbrook, later providing a number of members for the Wanderers club. The Old Boys team were founded in 1876 and entered the F.A. Cup in the same season, actually appearing alongside the school side. Old Foresters went on to play in two F.A. Cup Quarter-Finals before the turn of the century. In 1882 the school grounds hosted a Quarter Final tie against Marlow. To the visitor today, the school buildings are not as grand as might be expected.

The pitches are certainly well located, positioned down a long footpath through a wooded area. Arriving at a beautiful and well grassed field, there is a grass marked running track, a hockey pitch and 2 full-size pitches away to the right. The main pitch is not roped-off even when a crowd might warrant it – like the 100 or so that turned up for the 2005 Arthur Dunn Cup Semi-Final with Old Brentwoods. The players change in quite basic facilities in a small window-less pitch roofed building set back from the pitch.

Below*: A rare crowd assembles at*
The Park in April 2005.
Bottom*: The basic changing facilities.*
Very unbecoming of F.A. Cup Quarter-Finalists!

Old Lions F.C.

The Player's Club, Leigh Road, East Ham.
To coincide with the 2006 World Cup, Carlsberg filmed a TV advert here, featuring former England internationals under the guise of the Old Lions, playing pub football with Bobby Robson as their manager. The team was 1. Peter Shilton 2. Des Walker 3. Terry Butcher 4. Jack Charlton 5. Stuart Pearce 6. Peter Reid 7. Bryan Robson 8. Alan Ball 9. Bobby Charlton 10. Peter Beardsley 11. Chris Waddle.

They are seen dragging themselves to the ground on a Sunday morning, larking in the changing rooms and then emerging to face a clearly stunned Dog & Duck team. Turning on the style they romp to a 5-0 victory with goals from Beardsley, Butcher, Waddle, Robson and B. Charlton, before retiring to the pub for a well-earned pint. (Incidentally, the advert appears to show six goals, but Carlsberg say it is five....perhaps a dodgy Sunday lino ruled one out?)

For a few years prior to the advert shoot, the condition of the pitches had deteriorated and the grass was allowed to overgrow, although the goalposts on both pitches had remained in place. The iron gate entrance at the end of Leigh Road had only recently lost an impressive sign that stretched across the brick pillars and had read 'The Player's Club'. An insignificant sign on the wall to the right reveals that the ground is currently owned by British Gas PLC, formerly having been known as the North Thames Gas Sports Ground.

The pitch-roofed and weather-boarded social club is fronted by a brick pavilion extension with the whole ground being dominated by a huge gas holder, and at the other end of the pitch there is an electricity pylon too. The ground was exclusively used for cricket as far back as the early 1950s. This venue is a former home of London APSA, at a time when they were known as Ahle Sunnah.

Old Parkonians F.C.

Redbridge Sport & Leisure Centre,
Forest Road, Barkingside.

In 1902 a teacher at Park Higher Grade School in Ilford formed a football team for the benefit of both players and teachers. Despite pressure to become an 'open' club, members can still only be old boys from what is now known as Ilford County High School.

The Leisure Centre runs alongside Fairlop Station, on the Central Line. By following the driveway, the pavilion of the club comes into view on the left. This has been home to both the football and cricket clubs since 1993. The pavilion incorporates changing rooms, bar and function suite. It sits directly behind the near goal and provides an excellent view from its large glass windows. Sensibly these are shuttered when the ground is unattended, as is the adjacent scoreboard. A deep overhanging roof provides some cover from the elements. There is a low wooden barrier set back from the right hand touch line but this is to keep cars off the pitch as they wind their way around to the nearby ground of Frenford Senior F.C.

The club runs seven teams, with the firsts in the Southern Amateur League. For the 1920/21 season Old Parks won promotion to the senior division of this famous old league, and for four glorious seasons they rubbed shoulders with the likes of Ipswich Town. They also entered the Essex Senior Cup. During this period the club were playing at Gordon Fields in Gordon Road, Ilford except for 1921/22 when they were at Buntingbridge Farm, Barkingside. 1926 to 1988 was spent at Barkingside Recreation Ground (see Crowmill F.C.). Between 1988 and 1993 they were on the adjacent Oakfield Playing Field pitch.

Below, top right: *The covered area directly behind the goal. The shutters lift on matchday to provide viewing from the bar.*

Old Parmiterians F.C.

Douglas Eyre Leisure Centre, Coppermill Lane,
Walthamstow.

This old sports ground is administered by the London Playing Fields Foundation. Behind the large leisure centre block there was formerly a railed-off grass pitch which was used by the reformed Ilford F.C. in the London Spartan League in 1990/91, and later by Clapton Villa F.C. in the same competition. That has since been replaced by a floodlit and fenced-in Astroturf pitch. Beyond this stretches an area with many pitches which are in almost constant use at weekends. The No. 1 pitch is located here. It is not railed or even roped-off these days, but is distinguishable by two wooden dugouts that back onto the wall.

The chief occupant is Old Parmiterians F.C. of the Amateur Football Alliance. They are over 100 years old and run eight league teams and three veteran sides and a sister club of the same name who are based at Parmiters School, Garston in Hertfordshire, playing in the Herts County League.

In May 2006 Mauritius Sports F.C. hired out the main pitch here for their Middlesex County League Premier Division fixture with Stonewall. Despite a larger than usual attendance, the pitch was not roped-off for the occasion. Their usual base in Tottenham was unavailable.

Phoenix Youth (Leyton) F.C.

Drapers Field, Temple Mills Lane, Stratford.
Here is a forgotten venue with a real identity crisis. It also answers to just Drapers or Drapers Sports Ground. The address was once more commonly Gordon Road, Leyton (where the entrance is) but also Leyton High Road, which runs alongside.

Former residents, London Spartan Leaguers Walthamstow St. Mary have had a complicated history. Originally Islington St. Mary's, at one stage they merged with Walthamstow Trojans rebranding as Walthamstow St. Mary's. They then became St. Mary's (Islington) and then back to Islington St. Mary's. As Walthamstow St. Mary's they played here in 1994/95 in the London Spartan League Division 2. Ollerton F.C. had spent the previous season in the same division at this venue.

There is a two-storey brick pavilion which has most of the windows boarded-up with a covered area built in at the front. A grass bank stretches along the High Road side of the pitch with two pitches side by side parallel to that road. This ground looks to have potential, particularly if it could be enclosed on the High Road side, where there is only a mesh fence.

Snaresbrook F.C.

Snaresbrook F.C.

Nutter Field, Nutter Lane, Wanstead.
Immediately after the war Snaresbrook United were accorded senior status by the Essex County F.A. and placed into the Eastern Section of the hastily re-assembled London League for the 1945/46 season. This first post-war season was a difficult one, and the club pulled out of the league with three games to go, never to return to senior football. The final three matches were awarded to their opponents, rather than their entire record being expunged so at least they have the distinction of appearing in the final league table – in 8th position.

At this time there was a pitch-roofed pavilion at one end of the ground. This had a small central gable on the roof with a clock on it, and an area of cover underneath which was supported by four brick columns at the front, standing to the right of the cricket scoreboard. Fast-forward sixty years and that scoreboard is still there but the pavilion has been replaced by a more modern version, set back a little further than its predecessor, behind the left hand goal.

The football pitch is pinned up against the far side on slightly less undulating land than elsewhere. There is no room to expand at either end and the small pitch runs right up to the pavilion. Given that the old one was further forward the pitch must previously have been too short. Spectator comforts are provided by four bench seats that are lined up in front of the large glass windows and patio doors. There are no dugouts and no rope is required around the pitch to keep the crowds back for Essex Business Houses League Division Three games.

Below: *An OS map of the ground in 1939.*

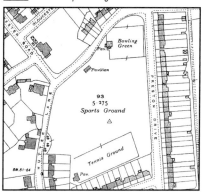

Tottenham Hotspur F.C. Academy teams

Spurs Lodge, Luxborough Lane, Chigwell.

The luxury facility now owned by Tottenham and known as Spurs Lodge was formerly the London Polytechnic Sports Ground. It has since changed beyond all recognition and has six full-size grass pitches, four intermediate and mini-size grass pitches, one full-size floodlit artificial pitch which can be covered in winter, one artificial surface indoor area, a fully equipped remedial gymnasium, fully equipped treatment rooms, shower and changing facilities and a canteen.

During the week the Spurs first team train here although the nearest the public get is to see the under-18s on Saturday mornings in the F.A, Premier Academy League. The first pitch visible on the left as you travel down Luxborough Lane is a full-size railed off grass pitch. The surround is grass rather than concrete and this slopes away, down toward the single storey brick complex in which the changing and other facilities are housed. The car park and entrance immediately beyond this is protected by a sentry box and barrier.

Top: The railed off grass pitch, and indoor facilities.
Above: The dugouts and camera gantry.

Below: The crowd watch an Academy match from the small roped off section.
Photos: Roger Adams

Further down the lane there is a left turn that leads to a car park. On the far right side of that is the pitch used for Academy fixtures. Houses back onto the left side, and this is where a length of rope stretches for just half of the pitch, provided a very limited amount of space for the hardy few. Spectators are not allowed behind either goal or on the other side, where there are two six seat dugouts separated by a video camera gantry. Programmes or teamsheets are no longer issued here.

Loughton F.C. played here in 1988/89 for their first season in the Ilford & District League, and returned to the ground as a London Spartan League Division Two team in 1992/93. However, after finishing bottom they disbanded at the start of the following season. Club founder member Keith Campen recalls his team's time at the ground: "I recall that there were three pitches. The pavilion complex was mainly wooden, including changing rooms with showers down the corridor. A licenced bar was on site, but not always available. We were permitted to put a rope around the pitch for 92/3 in the LSL. When we played there the pitch we used was adjacent to the motorway and Luxborough Lane. I believe there is now an astroturf pitch on it."

Tottenham may not be here for the long term. In 2005 they approached Enfield Council and the Lee Valley Regional Park Authority about developing a world class training facility and academy on the land behind Myddelton House, and a new community building providing education, sporting and community support programmes on the Bulls Cross sports ground. The land was designated green belt land so the outcome was never likely to be successful but gave out a clear signal of intent for the future.

Westhamians F.C.

Fairlop Oak Recreation Ground,
Fairlop Road, Hainault.

The sports ground, under various titles, has been in use since pre-WWI days, and once boasted a number of pavilions. Two very large ones stood on opposite sides of the pitches, housing multiple changing rooms. These were swept away in 2001, along with some of the pitches, and have been replaced with a smart new brick changing block and a number of floodlit all-weather ball courts for the mushrooming Powerleague 7-a-side franchise. The new building covered the area where a third substantial pavilion had been located, nearer the road.

The site is under the overall auspices of the London Playing Fields Society. In the summer of 2003 the National 5-A-Side Cup was taken away from Hackney Marshes and played at this venue. Utilising the artificial pitches, rather than marking out a series of grass ones limited the number of seats that could be installed compared to previous seasons. Temporary uncovered seats were erected on two sides of the No.1 pitch, providing seating for 800.

More recently, £150,000 has been invested here in two state of the art 7-a-side "rubber crumb" pitches. These "Third Generation" pitches are FIFA-approved and are widely used by professional clubs for training purposes. The unique rubber crumb top surface coupled with a rubber, sand and stone base is widely acknowledged as the closest artficial surface to real grass.

Essex Olympian League football returned to the sports ground at the start of 2005/06 when Westhamians F.C. moved up from the EBHL. Founded in 1925 as the West Ham Secondary Old Boys Club, they changed their name to Old Westhamians in 1928. The members were all former pupils of the West Ham Secondary School, subsequently Stratford Grammar School, and now the Stratford School. The club only became 'open' to outsiders in the 1980s. They moved out for the first two post-war seasons, to the Memorial Grounds at Canning Town, because Fairlop was still covered with anti-aircraft guns. Their pitch runs parallel to the fencing along the Powerleague pitches and is surrounded by a thin blue rope on match days. Two technical areas are marked out on the grass but there are no dugouts.

Technical areas for EOL games in Westhamians first season in the EOL

Below: *The main stand erected in 2003 on the car park area, for the 2003 National 5-A-Side Cup*

Also resident at this ground, but on one of the distant outer pitches, are Leyton County Old Boys F.C. This club were formed in 1932, making them the second oldest of many teams here. They compete in the Amateur Football Combination, a merger of the Old Boys Football League and the Southern Olympian Football League. Other residents from the same league are London Hospital Old Boys and Davenant Wanderers. This area can justifiably be called a hotbed of Essex football. Within strolling distance are Manford Way and Leytonstone United's pitches. Frenford Senior and Old Parkonians are just the other side of the Central Line. Redbridge/Barkingside play just down the road and the old Spartan League venue at Elmbridge Sports & Social Club is also nearby. West Ham's Youth team play a mile or so away at Little Heath.

The video camera gantry and dugouts on the far side, to which spectators have no access, at the West Ham United F.C. Academy ground.

West Ham United F.C. Academy

Little Heath Sports Ground, Hainault Road, Romford.
The ground had previously been used by intermediate level clubs Caribbean International and Little Heath. The latter club had occupied a pitch that ran alongside the A12, which was just a hedgerow away. Ilford also played here briefly in the 1991/92 season. Today the ground comes alive on a Saturday morning when crowds occasionally reaching three figure crowds congregate for West Ham's academy team fixtures. The favoured pitch for the under 18 team is on the far side of the sports ground, furthest away from the A12. The far touchline runs alongside a hedgerow and the dugouts and a camera gantry can be found there. Spectators are restricted to standing behind a rope on the opposite side only. As one might expect, the pitches here are in immaculate condition and have led to West Ham preferring the facilities here to their own training ground at Chadwell Heath in recent years. There is a tea bar under cover by the changing room block. If the next pitch along is used, the cover here forms a convenient shelter when wet and can be used to watch the game from behind the goal. Spectators are allowed access to the comforts of the nearby school's toilet facilities rather than use the ones in the changing blocks. Programmes are issued for competitive U16 and U18 fixtures.

West Ham United F.C. Training Ground

Saville Road, Chadwell Heath.
The club has plotted its ups, and frequent downs, from the Chadwell Heath training ground for many years. Supporters will tell you that it was here that Manager Ron Greenwood developed the talents of Bobby Moore, Geoff Hurst and Martin Peters which would 'win the World Cup' for England in 1966. Each of the full-size grass pitches were once accompanied by large brick spectator shelters alongside a touchline but these were removed in the early 1980s. Still visible on the mainline from Liverpool Street station, there is a large indoor sports hall, decked in club claret, and a floodlit all-weather court. Out of view of the trains, offices are situated in a number of outbuildings behind the hall. Of the remaining pitches the one that backs onto the sports hall is surrounded by photogenic boards reminding onlookers that Reebok provide the kit. A video camera gantry has previously stood on the East touchline, although it was no longer there in May 2006.

The ground is inconspicuous within the locality. At the end of Saville Road WHUFC in spelled out in gold on two iron gates and a board states that in deference to the neighbours players would not stop on the way out to sign autographs. It is possibly with the local residents in mind that the club stopped using the ground for youth team games a few years back and now play their Academy fixtures at Little Heath. Training sessions are not open to the public except on Tuesdays and Thursdays during school holidays.

Other grounds

Bancroft F.C.
Bancroft RFC, Buckhurst Way, Buckhurst Hill.
The EBHL team plays on a pitch at the 24-acre site of a Rugby Union side that once was a very successful football team! Old Bancroftians F.C. were formed in 1894 as the old boys team of Bancrofts School in Woodford Green. They won the Essex AFA Senior Cup in 1910,11 & '14, and the Old Boys Cup in 1922,3,4,6 & '27. The school stopped playing football at around this time and switched codes to rugby, inheriting a ground at Loughton. In 1968 they moved to the present ground, and changed to the current name in 1973. The current football club was formed in 2000 and operates independently of both the rugby club and the school, utilising a side pitch.

Beaumont Athletic F.C.
Weavers Field, Derbyshire Street, Bethnal Green.
Bethnal Green United considered this park in 2004 when looking for a ground to use in the top division of the MCL. Two small pitches marked out at either end. During the 2005/06 season these were used by Beaumont Athletic of the EBHL, Vallance Hackney Marshans F.C. Beaumont were elected to the ESL in 2006, moving to Mile End Stadium.

Clapton F.C. Reserves
West Ham Park, Ham Park Road, London.
This beautiful park was officially opened on 20 July 1874 and today there are two cricket squares, twelve tennis courts, a bandstand, a rounders pitch, large children's playing area, a paddling pool…and two football pitches. There is also a rough and ready 'all-weather' pitch, in the truest East End sense, meaning it is dusty shale. Clapton Reserves play the majority of their Ilford & District League games here, on one of two pitches that are somewhat superior to the one at The Old Spotted Dog. The changing facilities are provided within the huge cricket pavilion which has both a roof for spectator cover and a front retaining wall. While the building is used by the footballers, sadly the cover is not as the first of the two pitches is a long walk away.

East Ham Baptist F.C.
Flanders Playing Field, Melbourne Road, East Ham.
With great pride Flanders Playing Field was once described as Newham's 'Wembley' or even 'Lords'! The large pavilion in the NW corner has long gone and been replaced by a series of windowless containers. East Ham United looked at moving here in 1999.

Glendale F.C.
Clayhall Park, Long Wood Gardens, Ilford.
Formerly known as Clayhall Recreation Ground, this ground was home to Barkingside F.C. between 1921-29. The park is a short walk North West of Gants Hill underground station and the red-brick cricket pavilion looks old enough to have been used during his time. Glendale F.C. of the I&DL play on a pitch near the cricket square.

Globe Rangers F.C.
George White Sports Ground, Billet Road, Walthamstow.
The compact ground is hidden away behind a tall wall, although there is a name board, declaring them to be a member of the AFA even though they currently ply their trade in the EBHL. There is a brick pitched roof building with changing rooms alongside the pitch to the right, with 2 green dugouts on the opposite side. A small bar area is adjacent to the facilities and there is very limited space for cars.

Loughton F.C.
Former home - Roding Valley Playing Fields, Roding Rd.
Loughton F.C. began life as Goals Incorporated F.C., an under-11 side, in February 1965. They became Loughton Boys F.C. in the summer of that year and played at this ground until 1990. A men's side was formed in 1988, joining the Ilford & District League and playing at Luxborough Lane, Chigwell (see under Tottenham Hotspur F.C.) in that season and the Norwegian Ground at Jenkins Lane, Barking the following year. In 1990 the current ground at Avondale Close was purchased.

While based here in 1981/82 Loughton Boys had an extraordinary run to the 3rd Round Proper of the F.A. Youth Cup before losing 4-0 to Watford. Their victors went on to lift the trophy after beating Manchester United in the Final. Their home cup games were played under floodlights at the Stonards Hill home of Epping Town F.C. These playing fields still exist, with the far end backing on to the current ground. During Loughton's stay they used the brick-built changing rooms and put a rope up around the nearest pitch for their Essex Intermediate League seasons between 1990-92.

Midland F.C.
Brittania Sports Ground, Billet Road, Walthamstow.
This Ilford & District League club's ground is located up a lane off Billet Road. The signpost on the main road points to the home of Forest Rovers F.C., who also use the ground. The facility is a basic field.

Newham United F.C.
Langdon School, Langdon Crescent, East Ham.
Newham United were formed as recently as 2002 and compete in the EBHL. They play on a pitch at Langdon School close to the A406, which is as basic as you would expect it to be. Changing facilities are in the school, with players then trekking across to the pitch. The status of the club dictates that there is currently no need for dugouts, although the pitch has been roped-off from time to time for cup ties. The pitch had previously been used by Old Esthameians, from when they entered the Southern Amateur League in 1971. That club played several F.A. Vase games on this ground in the 1980s, although the pitch ran at right angles to the current one and a small building in the outfield, which still exists, was used for changing facilities.

Old Egbertian F.C.
Peter May Sports Centre, Wadham Lodge, Walthamstow.
Formed in 1928 they were started by former pupils of St Egberts College at the Ridgeway, Chingford. The relationship between the College and the Football Club broke down in 1968 when the Club lost the use of the pitch at the bottom of Kings Head Hill.

There is a second prominent club at this sports ground. Clapton Orient Womens F.C. were formed back in the 1992-93 season by Leyton Orient F.C.'s Community Sports Programme. This was one of the first community schemes to develop women's and girls' football in the local area. Clapton Orient is Leyton Orient's pre-war name and reflects the area where they used to play.

Tottenham Hotspur Ladies have also played here. The sports ground itself has been around for many years, once known as the London Transport Sports Ground (and including Walpole Athletic F.C. among its long list of clubs), and later Wadham Lodge (not to be confused with the ground of the same name used by Waltham Forest F.C.). It has recently had a multi-million pound makeover with the help of £5m of lottery funding and now has an indoor sports hall and artificial pitch. The football pitches are away from the viewing area and there are no specific spectator amenities, dugouts or even a rope around the pitches.

Old Ludlows F.C.
Elmbridge Sports & Social Club, Forest Road, Hainault.
Old Ludlows F.C. are the highest placed club of several who use the run down facilities at Elmbridge Sports & Social Club, albeit in Division One of the Ilford & District League. The venue was previously the London Transport Sports Ground. Hackney Downs F.C. and Newmont Travel F.C. played here in the London Spartan League in the 1980s and early 1990s. When Hackney Downs were promoted to Division One they planned to rail off the pitch but this never happened. The whole ground today appears neglected. There is a large car park in front of the changing room and social club block and pitches behind and to the sides of the buildings. The one to the left was roped off for LSL football but with no other spectator comforts.

Pembury Knights F.C.
Hackney Downs, Downs Park Road, Hackney.
The Downs have been associated with sport since horse racing was introduced here in 1733. Cricket was also played for many years. The first recorded football match was between Sky Rockets and Oakfield in 1872. Clapton F.C. began life here in 1877 as Downs F.C., using The Downs Hotel as their HQ. This is still an open space today and is bordered by Downs Road, Queensdown Road and Downs Park Road in Upper Clapton. There is still a football pitch in the park, used by Pembury Knights, although the Spartan League club of the same name played elsewhere.

Rainham Working Men's Club F.C.
Rainham Recreation Ground, Upminster Road South.
Rainham Town F.C. played here after WWII from 1945-48 while in the South Essex League, moving out only when their new home at Deri Park was ready. This ground is adjacent to the spacious Rainham Working Mens Club. The driveway from the main road leads past the club with the pitch to the right. The playing area is very cramped with the other three sides surrounded by a fence and buildings. There is no room for even a rope on these sides, leaving spectators to jostle for position with the cars. The club have played here for many years, once in the SEL, but these days in EBHL.

Ryan F.C.
Parmiters Sports Ground, Nelson Road, Chingford.
Ryan were formed in 1994/5, originally as Beaumont FC in the Ilford & District League. After one season Richard Williams took control and re-named the club after his son. The club won promotion from Division Three through to the top level. In 2003/04 the club amalgamated with Wanstead Town F.C. and Dalina F.C. and obtained intermediate status in the process, taking the WTFC's place in the EOL. That club had played at Blake Hall Sports Ground (see Old Esthameians), but Parmiters was retained. The flat-roofed clubhouse/pavilion is angled toward the cricket square. The football pitch is roped-off on matchdays. There is no spectator cover or dugouts.

Upminster F.C.
Hall Lane Playing Fields, Hall Lane, Upminster.
This open ground is flanked by trees on either side of the pitch. It is little more than a field during the week but at weekends the goals are put up and the pitch roped-off. The dressing room complex is a little way away, faces out onto the cricket square, and is heavily fortified. There are two metal benches alongside the pitch.

West Essex F.C.
The Rolls, Hickman Avenue, Highams Park, London.
The Rolls was used in the Spartan League by Newportonians between 1919-26. There is a modern brick pavilion looking out over one of two cricket pitches. The first team plays in the EBHL so there is no need to rope off the pitch except for home ties in the Essex Premier Cup.

West Ham United F.C. Community Pitch
Albatross Close, Beckton.
This amenity is approximately on the site of the former Beckton United ground, adjacent to the A13 flyover and the disused Beckton Dry Ski Slope. It is a floodlit U.E.F.A.-approved artificial surface, completed in early 2004. Enclosed in a tall standard wire mesh fence, the only hint of the ownership is the West Ham corner flags. The two storey changing room block sits outside the fence, and has a small (very small) cover attached to it, facing out toward the pitch. Canning Town have hopes of staging first and second team matches here in future. In May 2004 a Middlesex League First Division game was played here between Brazilian FSSC and Ealing Assyrians.

Plans and projects...

Aveley F.C.
Green Belt Project 1996.
In 1996 the club was approached by a building company who were looking to buy Mill Field. The club had eyes on a new site, also in Aveley, comprising 20 acres of designated green belt land. Negotiations broke down, but it is unlikely that permission would have been granted for the new ground anyway.

Bethnal Green United F.C.
Meath Gardens, Roman Road, Bethnal Green 2004.
The club considered this venue during the summer of 2004, when looking for an enclosed Middlesex County League Premier Division venue. This neglected park has little natural light, and the former changing room block has been knocked down.

Hornchurch F.C.
Upminster, Near A127 2004.
Frustrated by local opposition to develop Bridge Avenue, Hornchurch looked in 2004 at a possible site for a new ground along the A127 in Upminster.

Hornchurch F.C.
St. George's Hospital, Suttons Lane, 2004.
Later in 2004 Hornchurch were also said to be looking at this site. The hospital was to be replaced with housing, & possibly a football ground. The timescale to complete this project may have been too long to dovetail in with the club's plans.

Romford F.C.
Manor Road, Dagenham 2002.
Just south of Dagenham & Redbridge's Victoria Road ground, clubs in the Barking & Dagenham area were unhappy and youth club Dagenham United plan to develop a multi-sports arena.

Romford F.C.
Lower Bedfords Road, Harold Hill 2005.
In 2005 Romford applied for planning permission for a ground in Harold Hill. They had previously looked at over a dozen sites, including Five Oaks Lane in Hainault, Forest Lodge in Collier Row and Manford Way's current ground. This venture was on green belt land and had previously been looked at by both Collier Row and Hornchurch. It had a travellers' site on one side, a school on another and a notorious council estate opposite. The residents of the sole neighbouring street opposed the plans and matters have proceeded at a snail's pace.

Stratford – Olympic Stadium 2012.
At the heart of London's winning bid for the 2012 Olympic Games was an 80,000-seat stadium (image below) to be built at Marshgate Lane in Stratford. This would not feature in the 2012 football tournament, which would use other stadiums with the final taking place at Wembley Stadium.

When the plans were first aired West Ham expressed an interest in moving there after the games. Plans were laid out for 55,000 temporary seats to be removed after the Paralympic Games had been completed, leaving behind a 25,000-seat athletics arena.

The Hammers were told that it would not be possible to renege on the promises made and that football was out of the question. However, subsequent to the games being won rumours persisted that Tottenham Hotspur were also looking at the stadium. They too were told 'no chance!'

In early 2006 Lord Coe stated that the Olympic Committee had never ruled out football having a future there, and suddenly it seemed that West Ham were back in the frame. There are sure to be many twists and turns leading up to the Games but if either of these Premier League clubs were to relocate to Stratford they would certainly demand a larger capacity than 25,000. My money is on West Ham moving in at the start of 2013/14.

Computer graphic images illustrate the concept (below), and a version of the future stadium was 'brought to life' in an episode of Doctor Who on 24th June 2006.

Last but not least...

St. Vincents F.C.
Leyton County Ground (The Lyttelton Ground),
Crawley Road, Leyton.

The County Ground in Leyton is best known as a former home to Essex County Cricket Club but has been used for football for over 100 years. It has the distinction of once being used to host an Arsenal home game in the Football League, and was also home to the Casuals. The poet Alfred Lord Tennyson even wrote a poem about this great historical venue, although perhaps not his finest work!

Essex C.C.C. moved to the ground from Brentwood in 1885, and stayed until 1933. In 1886 there were two international fixtures and Essex beat the Australians on the ground in 1899, the West Indies in 1906 and New Zealand in 1927. The ground at the time was known as the Lyttelton Ground, after Lord Lyttelton, the previous owner. It cost £12,000 to get the venue into shape and a year later a further £3,500 was spent, mostly on the elaborate pavilion which is still the focal point of the ground today. This had six long rows of benches in front of it and was fronted by a white picket fence.

To the left of this was a long grandstand with a raised tier and pitched roof. An additional lower tier was added to two-thirds of the stand, at the pavilion end. This section was given a taller and more distinctive roof. Spectators had to contend with eleven additional support columns as well as the same number that once formed the front of the original stand, but which had ended up in the middle. The seats were very uncomfortable and cushions were available for hire for a nominal sum.

By 1893 it was agreed that additional funds could be raised by allowing football to be played there. At the start of 1894/95 Leyton F.C. moved in, having just changed their name from Matlock Swifts. They stayed until the end of 1900/01.

Photo: Vince Taylor (1999)

Leyton County Cricket Club Ground c.1910 - note the stand just visible on the extreme left.

During this period the ground was also known as the Army Sports Ground. Toward the end of that season Woolwich Arsenal were in need of a home ground to stage league matches as their Manor Ground home in Plumstead had been closed for five weeks due to crowd disturbances. They had earlier hired out New Brompton's (now Gillingham F.C.) Priestfield Road ground in Kent but were looking for somewhere nearer home. The Lyttelton Ground fitted the bill nicely, and comfortably contained the 4,000 crowd that watched the 3-3 draw with Leicester Fosse on 9th March 1895.

Another famous club to make this club their home were The Casuals, who utilised many grounds in the London area and were here for a period directly before moving in with Corinthians F.C. in 1922 at the old Crystal Palace F.A. Cup Final venue. This led directly to Leyton moving back into the ground and the seven seasons that they spent back here up until 1929 were a golden era. They won the F.A. Amateur Cup in 1927 and 1928 and were losing finalists the following year. At this time the ground was equipped with a number of turnstiles to cope with the crowds.

The cricketers were also drawing plenty of attention to E10. In 1927 the first ever live broadcast of a cricket match was from Leyton. Then in 1932 Herbert Sutcliffe and Percy Holmes of Yorkshire formed a world record partnership of 555, which stood until bettered in 1976. At this time there were raised grass banks around the boundary and a small wooden cover with a very low roof at the High Road end, later giving way to an uncovered terrace. In 1933 the County Cricket Club moved out due to financial difficulties and declining membership numbers. They relinquished the lease, which was taken up by Metropolitan Police.

The cricketers then played at Southend, Colchester, County Ground Brentwood, Southend, Westcliff, Chelmsford and Ilford. Their HQ was at Duke St, Chelmsford.

For the 1936/37 football season 1st Coldstream Guards played here in their only Spartan League season.

The post war years have been far less eventful. A number of local schools used the ground for their sports days. Football at a moderate level has continued, although the chance of another top level club moving in disappeared when the grandstand was removed. Essex C.C.C. returned to play festival games in 1957, for which temporary stands and seating were erected. The very last of these was in 1977 against Glamorgan.

Photo: Vince Taylor (1999)

Above: The ground circa 1930.

Below: The scoreboard for the record breaking partnership in 1932

Above: An undated view of the ground showing the pavilion and stand.

Below: An OS map of the Leyton County Cricket Ground in 1939.

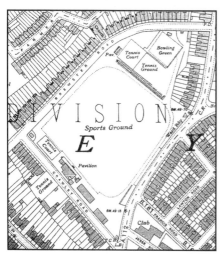

Leyton Youth Centre has since been sited on part of the old outfield and tennis courts, ruling out further top class games and also limiting the length of the football pitch. Leyton County played here for over twenty years, in the Intermediate Division of the Spartan League in the 1980s, and later in the Essex Intermediate League and London Intermediate League. By this time the seats in front of the pavilion had been removed and the concrete terracing on the High Road side (behind the goal) had also gone, as had the eight foot-high wall at the rear. Waltham Forest District Council decided to open up the ground by replacing the wall with railings so people could see in. They were advised that these should be no wider than a cricket ball but took no notice, having to fit a narrower set after a number of predictable mishaps!

The wall today sports a blue heritage plaque noting the world record opening stand. The two steps of terracing on the far side of the cricket arena were also removed, although this did have the benefit of freeing up room for a second football pitch on the site of the old practice nets. Despite the loss of status, stands and open seats, the ground is still very imposing and the old pavilion is relatively unchanged, with its two pitch roofed changing rooms on either end.

A visit to this 119 year old gem is highly recommended. Today the highest placed club using the ground is St. Vincents of The Ilford & District League Division One. Second Division Trelawny also use the ground, as do several Sunday League teams.

Name changes

A number of clubs featured in this book have changed their name at some point in their history. To aid future historians the various names used are listed below.

From	To
Ahle Sunnah	London APSA
Barkingside Boys Guild	Barkingside Old Boys & in the 1930's Barkingside.
Beaumont	Ryan. Incorporated Wanstead T & Dalina in 2003.
Briggs Motor Bodies	Briggs Sports, then merged with Ford Sports to become Ford United. Later re-branded as Redbridge.
Co-ordinated Traffic Services	Canning Town.
Eagle Park	Chadwell Heath, 1928/29 only.
Ford Sports	See Briggs Motor Bodies above.
Goals Incorporated	Loughton Boys 1965 and then Loughton in 1988. Not connected to Loughton Town or Loughton Athletic.
Hainault Labour Club	Manford Way.
KPG Tipples	Tower Hamlets.
Matlock Swifts	Leyton, then Leyton-Wingate; merged with Walthamstow Pennant & became Leyton Pennant; demerged toLeyton.
Orient	Clapton Orient in 1898, to Leyton Orient 1945, Orient 1966 & back to Leyton Orient in 1987 .
Parkhill	Chingford. Vaguely connected clubs include Chingford Town Wanderers, Chingford T, Chingford Utd.
Pennant	See Matlock Swifts / Leyton above.
Purfleet	Thurrock.
Snaresbrook United	Snaresbrook.
Sporting Club Henderson	Briefly became Harold Hill in 1995/96.
Three District (M.P.)	Three Area (M.P.) in 1980, Chigwell Police in 1986, & Metpol Chigwell in 1990's.
Upminster Wanderers	Hornchurch & Upminster in 1953, Hornchurch in 1960,re forming in 2005 as AFC Hornchurch.
Walthamstow Pennant	The 2003 club merged with Walthamstow Avenue 2000 in 2005 to become Walthamstow Avenue & Pennant 2000.
Walthamstow St. Mary's	Changed name to St. Mary's (Islington) in 1995, earlier merged with Walthamstow Trojans for a short period.
Walthamstow Trojans	To Trojan for final Spartan League Season in 1996/97.
West Ham Secondary OBC	To Old Westhamians in 1928 & Westhamians circa 1980.

Cross Reference...

The following clubs have played at various grounds listed in this book.

Club	Played at a ground listed under...
Ahle Sunnah (later London APSA)	Old Lions
Barking Rovers	Barking, Vicarage Field
Bealonians	play near Frenford Senior
Bethnal Green United	Clapton, London APSA, Hackney Marshes – East Marsh
Brazilian FSSC	West Ham Community Pitch, Waltham Forest
Briggs Sports	Dagenham & Redbridge, Victoria Road and Romford, Rush Green
BRSA	Faces
Caribbean International	West Ham United Academy
Clapton Orient Women	Old Egbertian
Clapton Villa	Hale End Athletic, Old Parmiterians
Craven	Brampton Park
Crown & Manor	Sporting Bengal United
Davenant Wanderers	Westhamians
Durning	London & Essex
East Ham United	London APSA
East Thurrock United	Heath Park
Eton Manor Reserves	Metpol Chigwell
First Coldstream Guards	St. Vincents
Ford United	Romford
Green & Silley Weir	Old Esthameians
Hackney Downs	Old Ludlows
Hackney Marshans	Beaumont Athletic
Ilford	Old Parmiterians
Ilford Wanderers RUFC	Leytonstone United
Leyton County	Hale End Athletic, St. Vincents
Leyton County Old Boys	Westhamians
Little Heath	West Ham United Academy
London Hospital Wanderers	Westhamians
Maidonians	Britannia
Mauritius Sports	Old Parmiterians
Melbourne Sports Reserves	London & Essex
Metropolitan Police	Metpol Chigwell
Millwall Athletic	Millwall Albion
Newmont Travel	Old Ludlows
Newportonians	West Essex
Old Blues RUFC	Manford Way
Ollerton	Phoenix Youth (Leyton)
Port Of London Authority	Faces
Rainham Town	Rainham Working Men's Club
Redbridge	Barkingside
Redbridge Forest	Dagenham & Redbridge
St. Bartholemews Hospital	Clapton
Singh Sabha	Hale End Athletic
Sporting Club Henderson	Mountnessing
Sterling Athletic	Dagenham & Redbridge
Tate & Lyle	Brampton Park
Tottenham Hotspur Ladies	Old Egbertian
Tower Hamlets	Sporting Bengal United
Trelawny	St. Vincents
Vallance	Beaumont Athletic
Walpole Athletic	Old Egbertian
Walthamstow Grange	Leyton
Walthamstow Pennant*	Hale End Athletic
Walthamstow Trojans	Leyton Orient Youth & Ladies
Wanstead Town	Old Esthameians
West Ham United Ladies	East Ham Baptist
Woodford Town	Clapton
Woolwich Arsenal	St. Vincents

Please note: It is not my intention to include lists such as those on pages 75 and 76 in future books. Mike Floate (Editor)